BALLPOINT ART PACK

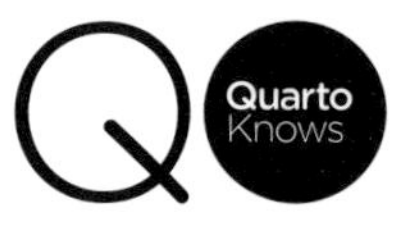

Quarto is the authority on a wide range of topics.

Quarto educates, entertains and enriches the lives of our readers—enthusiasts and lovers of hands-on living.

www.QuartoKnows.com

First published in the United States of America in 2016 by Quarry Books, an imprint of
Quarto Publishing Group USA Inc.
100 Cummings Center
Suite 406-L
Beverly, Massachusetts 01915-6101
Telephone: (978) 282-9590
Fax: (978) 283-2742
QuartoKnows.com
Visit our blogs at QuartoKnows.com

10 9 8 7 6 5 4 3 2 1

ISBN: 978-1-63159-127-3

The content for this kit was originally published in the book *The Art of Ballpoint* (Quarry Books 2016) by Matt Rota.

Design: Burge Agency
Cover type art: Joan Saló
Cover drawing: Matt Rota
Book back cover drawing: Matt Rota,
Joo Lee Kang
Case back cover drawing: Matt Rota
Inside cover: Joan Saló
Exercise artwork: Matt Rota

Printed in China

BALLPOINT ART PACK

CREATIVE TECHNIQUES AND EXPLORATIONS FOR DRAWING WITH AN EVERYDAY PEN

MATT ROTA

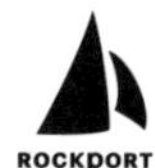
ROCKPORT

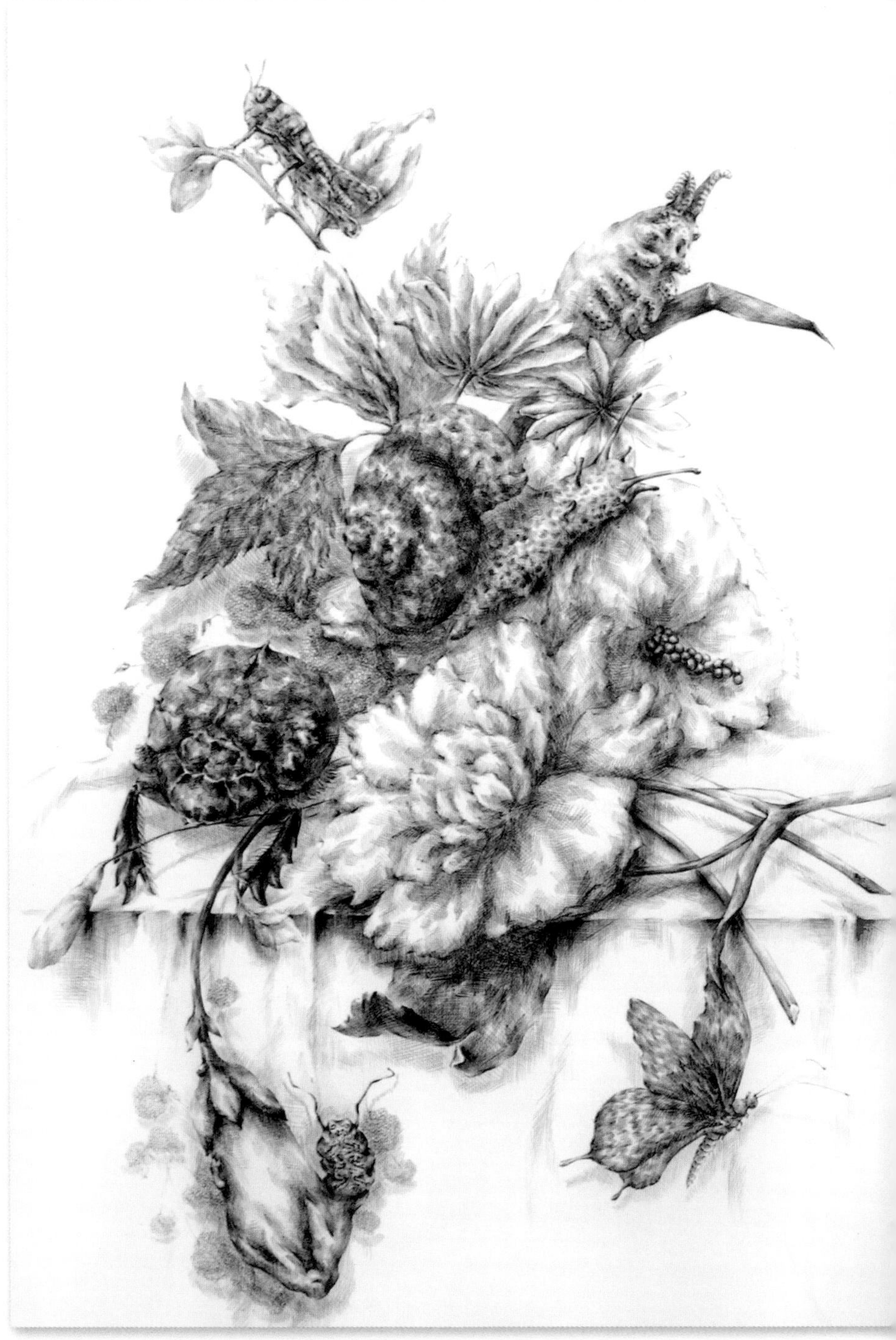

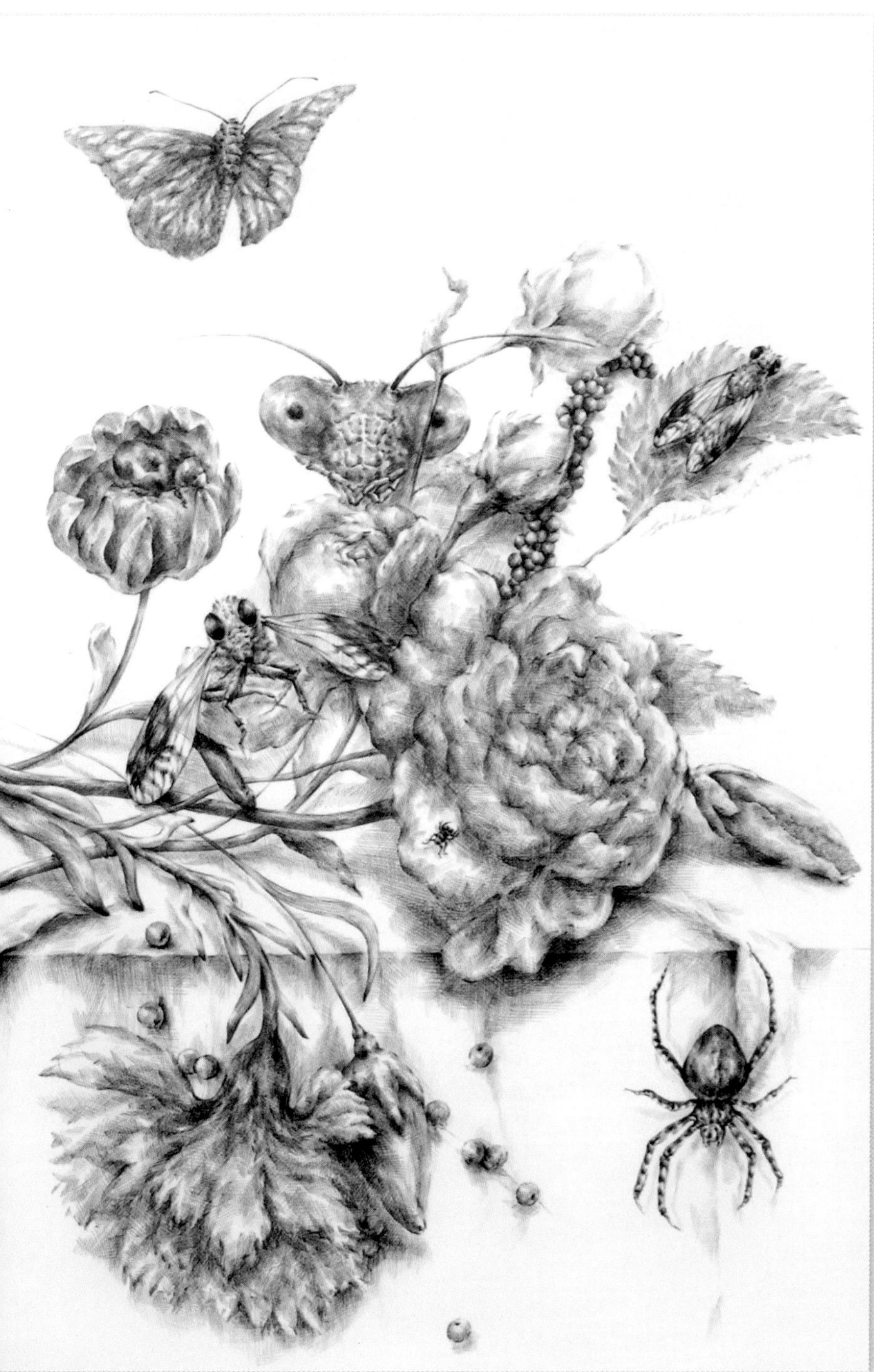

Image Highlight:

Joo Lee Kang
Still Life with Insects
#5 & #7, 2014
Ballpoint pen on paper
25 x 18 inches
(63.5 x 46 cm)

CONTENTS

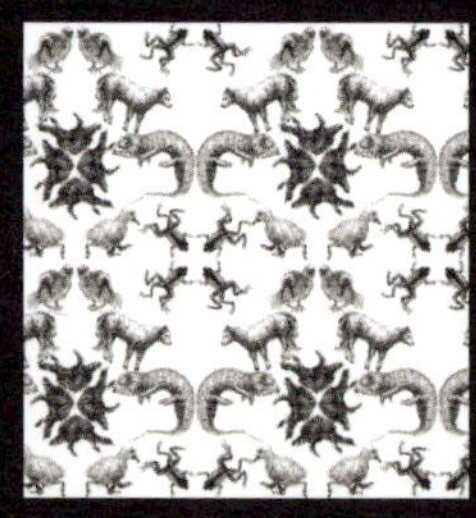

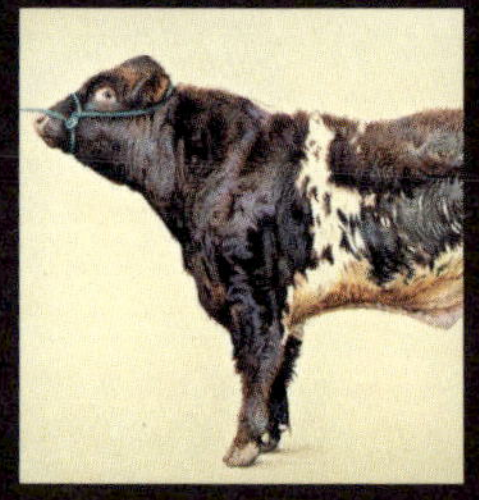

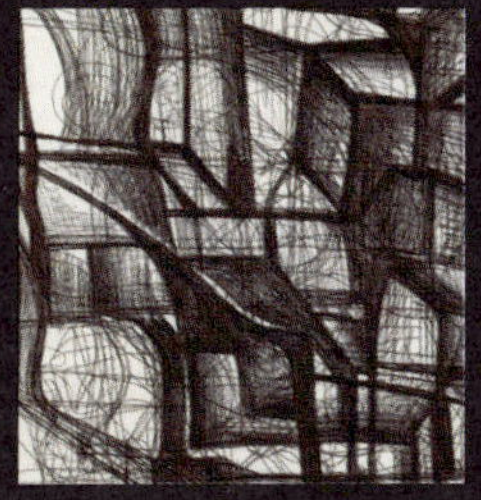

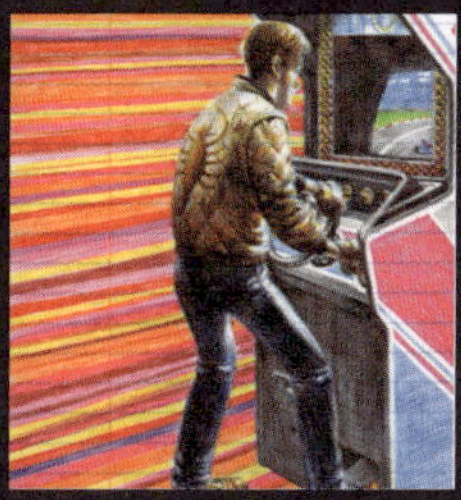

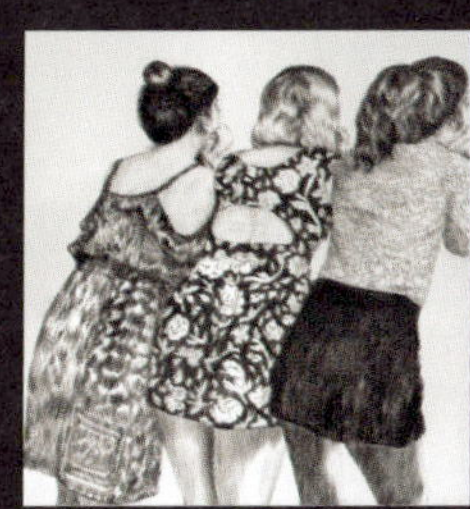

INTRODUCTION

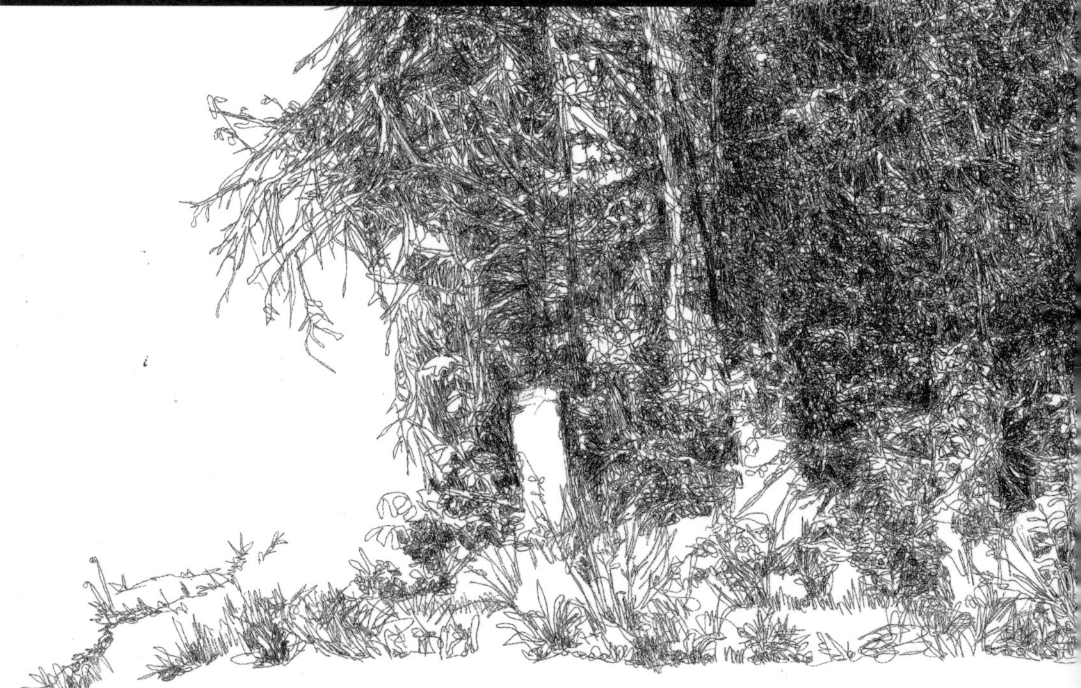

Hannah Chalew
Maxwell detail, 2014
Balloint pen on paper
26 x 40 inches
(66 x 101.6 cm)

WHY USE A BALLPOINT FOR ARTWORK?

Ballpoint drawing is often attractive to artists for usually one of two reasons. The first reason is that of convenience. Ballpoint pens are the most prevalent writing tool on hand at any moment, and by their sheer presence alone, they make their use as an art tool inevitable.

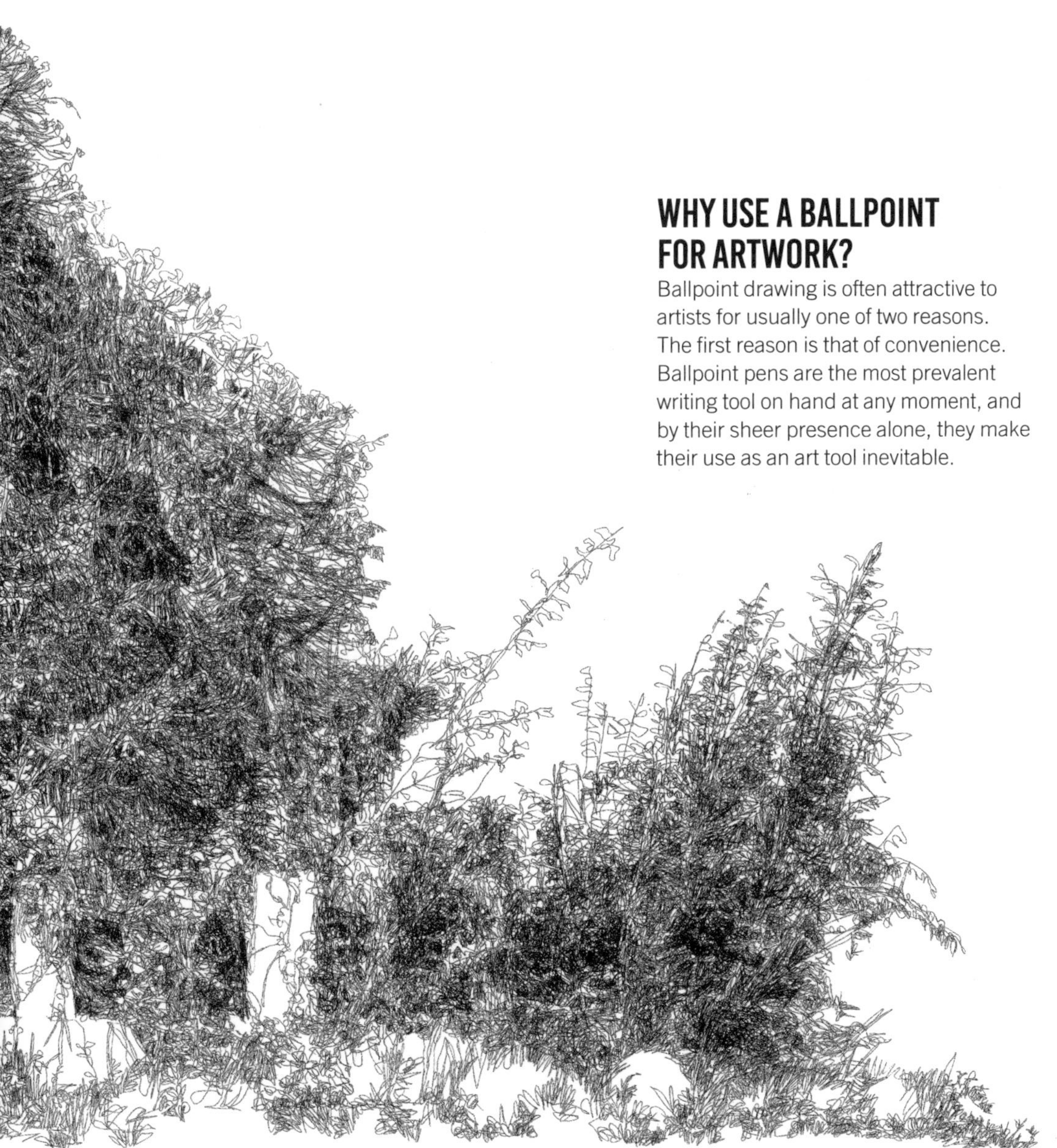

When the use is only convenience, it speaks to none of the qualities of the pen as a tool of expression, only to the lack of anything else present at the moment of desire and inspiration. But this mere convenience also conceals the secret power of the tool, of which the user may be unaware . . . imagine the lack of such abundance, a hotel room with no pen, when, late at night, an idea is stirred, a bar where, once inspiration strikes, there is no tool at arm's length that draws so easily on a napkin or paper menu. Imagine how many ideas would be lost without the direct connection that the ballpoint supplies from imagination to reality without any effort. With this convenience, the path from abstraction to reality has become like breathing, like a bottomless cup of water with which no one should ever be thirsty again. The invisibility of this convenience is so often taken for granted that the revelation of such abundance is relegated to the term *convenience*, assigning the tool a mediocrity that threatens to undermine its importance.

Imagine how many ideas would be lost without the direct connection that the ballpoint supplies from imagination to reality without any effort.

The second reason for the use of the tool can at times be equally invisible. This reason is relative to the pen's technical qualities, in the constant flow of ink, the convenience of not having to sharpen, dip, or refill the pen during the course of a drawing. The significance of this quality is often overlooked by artists born after the 1950s, when ballpoint pens replaced fountain pens and became like air. This quality facilitates a frame of mind in an artist, which, previous to the pen's invention, would have been impossible. The frame of mind is an unbroken focus, the ability to lose oneself in a drawing completely, a type of meditation that is seen so often in the art that comes from the pen. This focus, coupled with the fine fixed point of the pen, a tip that is limited to the thinnest mark, helps create the kind of drawing that demands focus. A ballpoint drawing by its very nature is detailed, intimate, and, as a result, almost always cerebral. It requires of the artist a patience that a pencil or a brush does not demand.

This is the mind-set that allows people to get lost in their work, whether it's a doodle, a sketchbook page, or a drawing the size of a wall or building. The drawing that comes from a ballpoint pen is labored and focused. It relies on the wrist more than the whole arm, and it's intimate even on a grand scale.

A ballpoint drawing by its very nature is detailed, intimate, and, as a result, almost always cerebral. It requires of the artist a patience that a pencil or a brush does not demand.

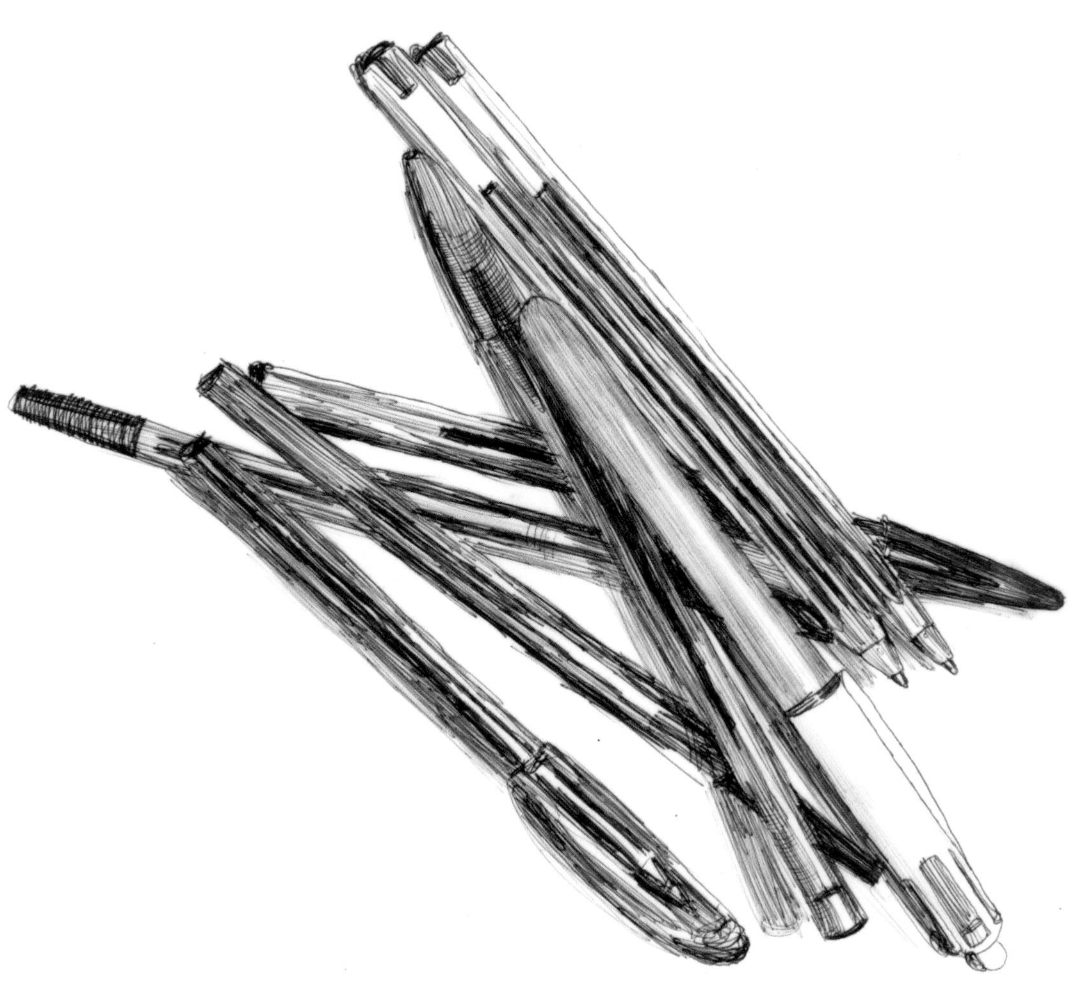

HOW A BALLPOINT PEN WORKS

The ballpoint pen is one of the most prominent, visible, and successful examples of a manufactured consumer product to come out of the postwar industrial age. The manufactured materials that constitute the pen include plastic for the barrel and ink cartridge (specifically, thermosetting plastic, or phenolic resins, plastics that remain permanently hard after being heated, molded, and cooled), brass for the tip, brass or aluminum for the construction of the body, and tungsten carbide for the ball. Ink, the most distinct and important innovation of the ballpoint pen, is made up of 40 to 50 percent dye and is combined with lubricants, thickeners, and preservatives, all of which are dispersed in oleic acid, castor oil, or sulfonamide plasticizer.

Brass is used because of its light weight and corrosion resistance, thermoplastic materials because of their hardness, but also their flexibility, and the tungsten carbide ball, where the tool's namesake comes from, is used for its resistance to warping. The surface of the ball is covered with thousands of tiny holes connected by tiny channels that allow the ball to retain ink within it, as well as spread the ink across its surface. The ink is the key to the pen's success; the story of the evolution of the pen is largely the evolution of the ink itself. The ink is thick and dries quickly so as not to smudge, but it is not too thick that it will clog the pen or dry up in the tube.

The ball was designed as a way of sealing the ink off from the air, which will dry it, and as a way of preventing the ink from leaking; its also the object that delivers the ink to the paper. In most cases, gravity delivers the ink to the tip, though in some cases, pressurized and spring-loaded piston designs are also used. Only the Fisher space pen is designed to be able to draw upside down; no other ballpoint model can accomplish this.

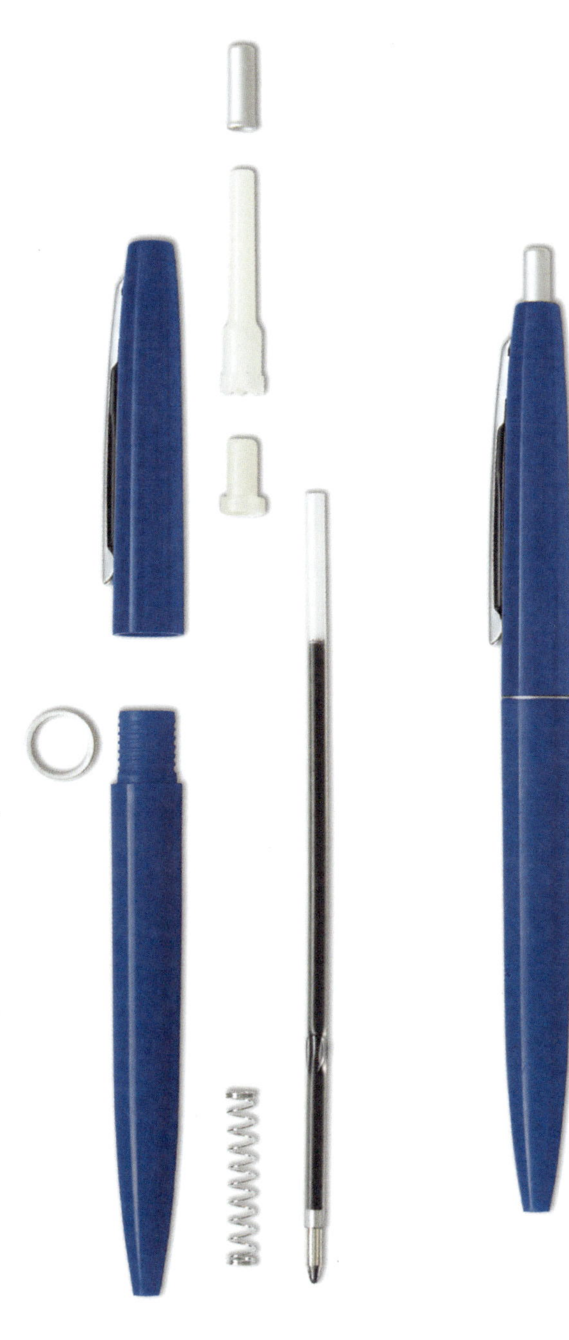

WHAT IS A PEN?

An anti-art tool

A tool that expresses logic and restraint

An attempt to recall adolescent abandon as a creative process

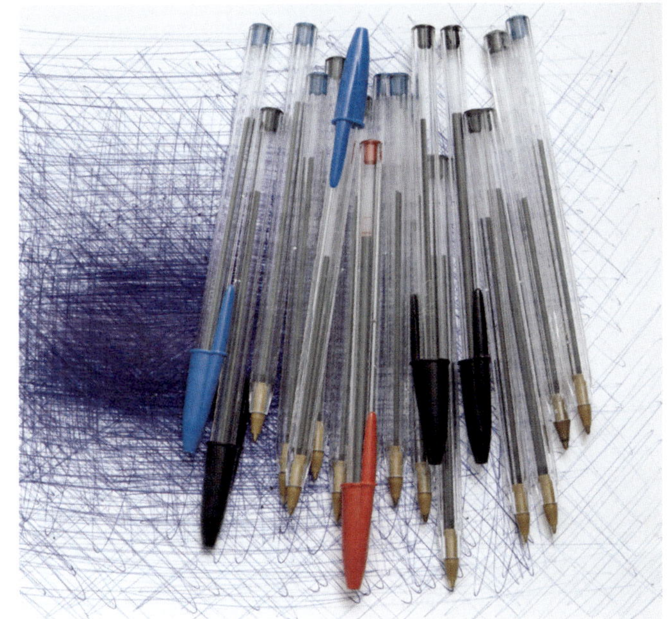

STATUS AS A TOOL

The attraction to the pen, beyond just its formal quality, has much to do with its status as a utensil for art. There is no consistent view or perspective but multiple interpretations of the tool. There is a group of thought that comes from its status as a nontraditional, anti-art tool; it has an outsider status. People who associate with this tend to relate to or are part of "outsider art," or lowbrow movements. This can be reflected in the subjects these artists choose, such as tattoos or reinterpretations of snapshots, ms, reproductions of sketches or graffiti designs, and other "nonart" subjects. The pen's association as lowbrow also encourages artists to use it as a tool to reinterpret classical or highbrow subjects, such as Lenny Mace's *Mona Lisa*.

The pen's status as an industrial-age tool, a product of manufacturing, is an attraction for others who view the pen as modern. The ballpoint can be seen as having associations with other forms of mechanical drawing tools, which negate personal expression in a minimalist sort of way by taking the ego out of the mark, forming a more perfect expression, a clarity of the modern industrial age; it is a tool that expresses logic and restraint and thus makes it elegant.

For others, it's a tool of nostalgia, used by artists with a carefree mentality toward drawing. The pen in this way is synonymous with innocence, recalling a doodle made during a phone call or a way to distract oneself during a high school lecture by scribbling in the margins of a notebook. The art that springs from this impulse by a mature artist is an attempt to recall adolescent abandon as a creative process.

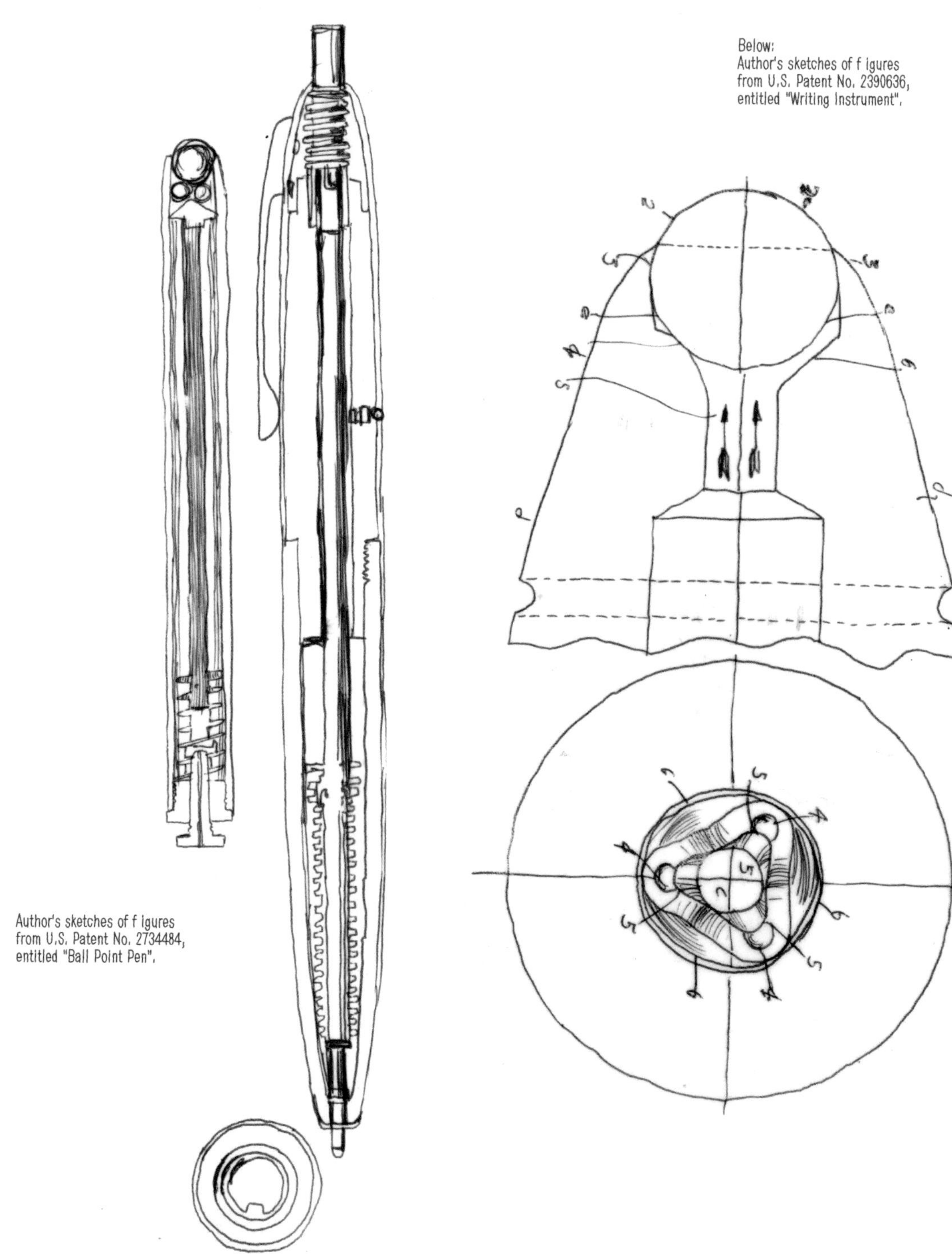

Below:
Author's sketches of figures from U.S. Patent No. 2390636, entitled "Writing Instrument".

Author's sketches of figures from U.S. Patent No. 2734484, entitled "Ball Point Pen".

A BRIEF HISTORY OF THE BALLPOINT

The first ballpoint model was patented by the American leather tanner and inventor John J. Loud, who had intended the tool to be used for marking and drawing on his leather products. The problem with the original design was the coarseness of the ball, which prevented it from drawing on delicate surfaces like paper. The ink also was a problem due to smearing.

After the initial patent was issued to Loud, more than 350 patents on similar ball-type pen designs were issued during the following 30 years, but none proved successful until Laszlo Biro's design, the problems always being with the ball size and ink viscosity. Ink was the primary focus of Biro's design; he was the first to try using newspaper ink. His design required free-flowing ink that dried quickly, but not within the tube or on the ball. The ink is largely dye based rather than pigment based so as not to clog the pen.

Laszlo Biro was born to a Jewish family in Hungary. He sought the help of his chemist brother Georg and secured the financial backing and business partnership of Andor Goy. The group set about developing the first functioning design of what would become the ballpoint pen. Biro displayed his pen at the Budapest International Fair in 1931. A modified design, patented by Biro and Goy in 1938, is more or less the design still used today.

Paralleling the development of the pen was the political transition and turmoil in Europe that would eventually lead to Word War II. By the end of 1938, anti-Jewish laws were going into effect, forcing the Biro family to flee. The brothers settled in Argentina and secured financing for new patents and a manufacturing plant.

The first commercial pens were marketed in 1944, and initially they were a failure. The design, relying on a gravity delivery system, did not deliver ink accurately to the tip unless the pen was held perfectly upright, so creating a steady flow was problematic. This design was updated with a capillary design. The ball was redesigned as a rough stainless steel ball, which gripped the paper better and better spread ink. This new improved model was marketed throughout the country with greater, but still limited, success.

One of the initial contacts the brothers had made in Buenos Ares was Harry Martin, a British accountant living in South America at the time. Martin was aware that at that time, the British Royal Air Force was having trouble with writing utensils at high altitudes; the fountain pen was prone to leaking, and the officers were looking for a new design good for keeping flight logs while in the air. Martin saw a potential solution in the ballpoint design. He met with the Royal Air Force representative in Buenos Ares, as well as the U.S. representative, whom upon seeing the pen had Martin flown to Washington to demonstrate it for the United States Air Force. From there he traveled to London to demonstrate it for the Royal Air Force. This led to the first major contract for Biro, with the British government ordering 30,000 pens.

Several innovators and manufacturers, including Eberhard Faber and Milton Reynolds, made improvements and refinements following the war.

Societe Bic was the company started in 1945 (at the time called Socit PPA) by Baron Marcel Bich. The company would go on to produce iconic brands of disposable razors, lighters, and ballpoint pens. Between 1949 and 1950, Bich would design the next major iteration of the ballpoint pen, adjusting materials and design to allow for a pen, eventually, that would be introduced to the U.S. market and sold for 19 cents apiece. Bich's innovation was to produce a high-quality pen in such great amounts as to keep the price as low as possible. It is said that Bich's pen can be considered one of the most successfully manufactured products of all time, with an estimated 14 million sold each day, and 100 billion sold globally since 1950 (the hundred billionth sold in September of 2006).

Bich's company would eventually become synonymous with low-cost, disposable, everyday products, such as the razor and the lighter, but the pen would be his most significant contribution to postwar Western culture. The impact of this idea is more profound than it may seem today, but considering the presence and availability of these objects to the point of near invisibility, it's hard to overstate the ballpoint's effect on contemporary society. Case in point: the BIC Crystal is included in the Museum of Modern Art's permanent collection. Features of the design include the see-through tube, made to allow the ink level to be visible, the hexagonal body modeled after a pencil, and a small hole in the side of the body to equalize pressure inside the pen. Recent models of the pen also feature a cap with a hole in the top, designed to prevent suffocation in the event the cap is inhaled.

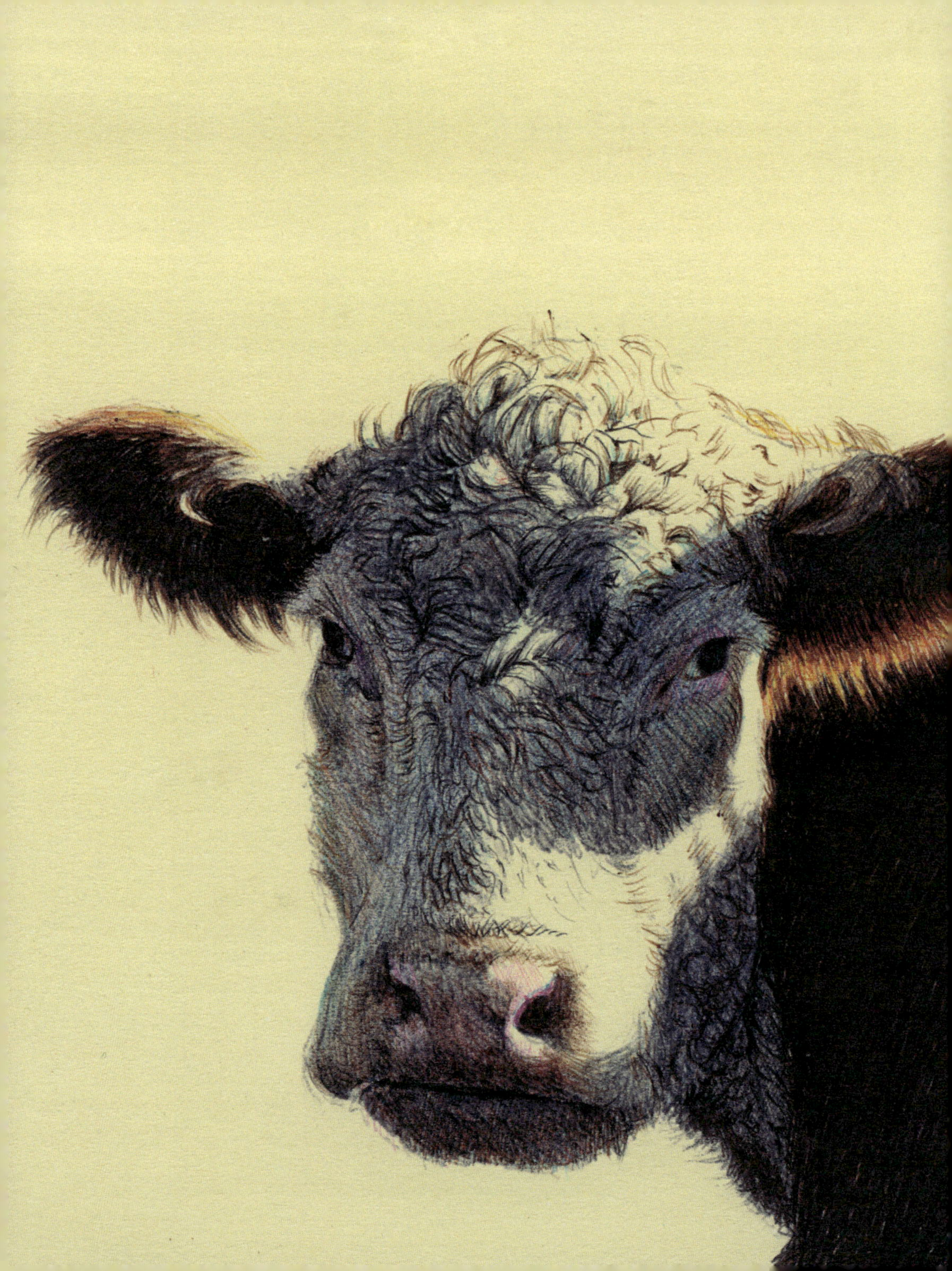

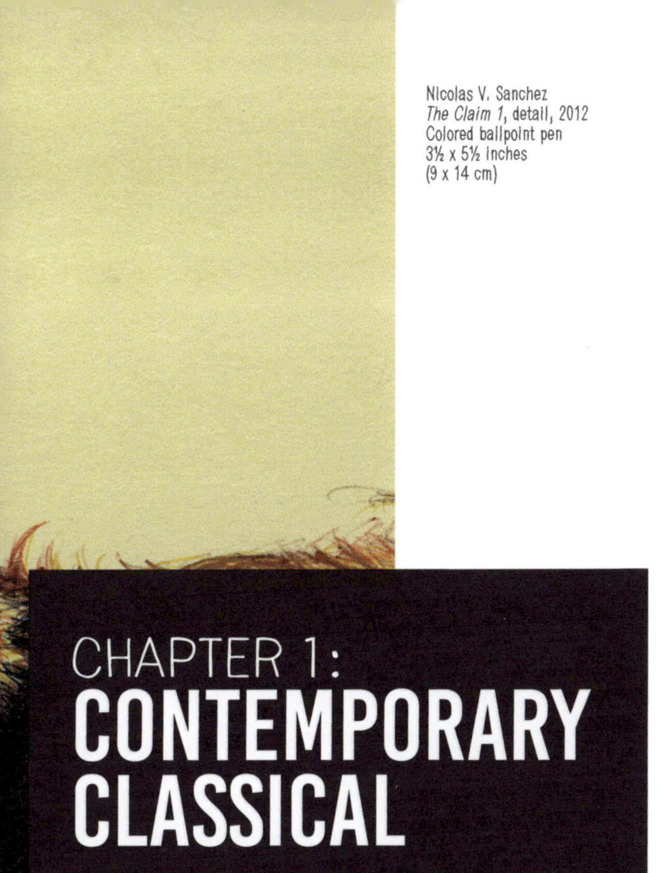

Nicolas V. Sanchez
The Claim 1, detail, 2012
Colored ballpoint pen
3½ x 5½ inches
(9 x 14 cm)

CHAPTER 1: CONTEMPORARY CLASSICAL

This chapter shares techniques that reference the long tradition of western European classical drawing through a combination of linear drawing and hatching for shadows and volume. The precision of a ballpoint lends itself well to translating these techniques into a modern context. The subject matter here is primarily figurative and uses drawing techniques typically relegated to pencil, charcoal, or traditional pen and ink.

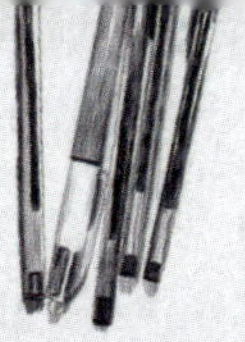

EXERCISE 1:

TYPES OF SHADING

THE OBJECTIVE OF THIS EXERCISE IS TO UNDERSTAND HOW DIFFERENT WAYS OF RENDERING AND SHADING CAN AFFECT THE SAME IMAGE.

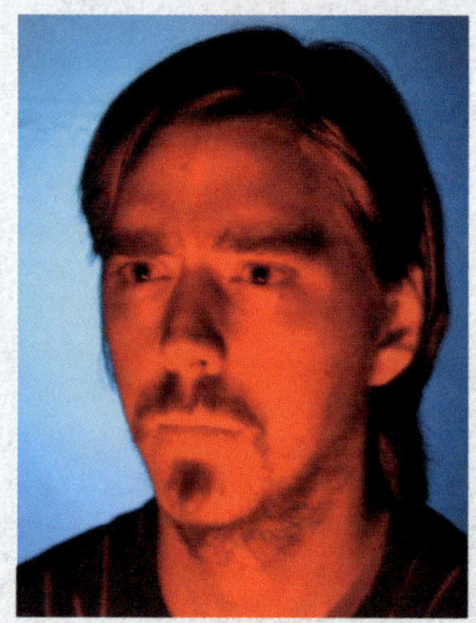

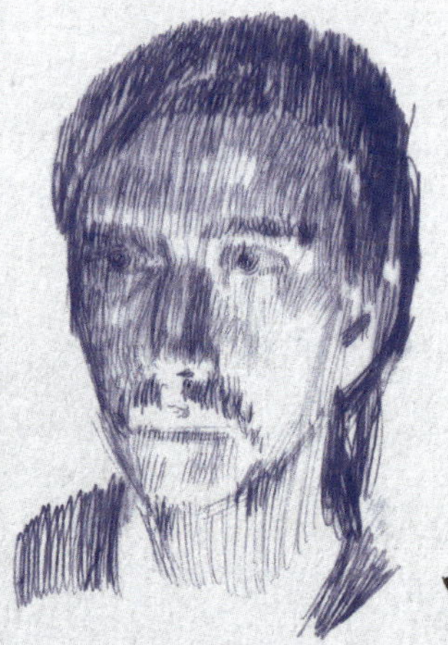

It is import before starting a drawing to have a clear understanding of the type of marks that will be used to describe the detail in the image. Each type of mark expresses a particular mood unique in its own right. Once the mark is decided, it is important to remain consistent within the drawing. Lines used in shading represent the way light travels across the surface of an object, so each type of mark gives the surface of an object a unique texture, and as a result, a unique energy. The different marks can be used to describe the same light, but with radically different feelings.

Using a mark that moves vertically down the face gives a sense that the light is moving downward; the lines pull the eye up and down, but not across the face. The surface of the face as a result looks long and smooth, and the singular motion adds a heightened sense of drama, or action, giving the feeling that the light is moving and causing the eye to move across the image quickly, unimpeded by a crosshatch. This gives a similar effect of raining, or a waterfall.

The lack of outline in this drawing also gives a softer feeling to the face, as if it were emerging from smoke, or some kind of atmosphere; the face appears less solid without any defining structural lines. This could give the impression of the face being a reflection in a mirror or water, for instance.

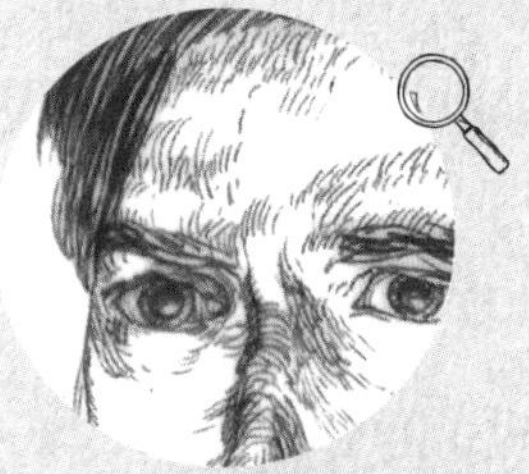

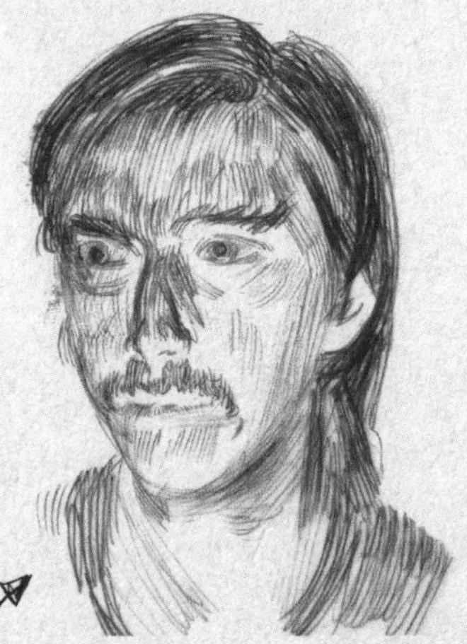

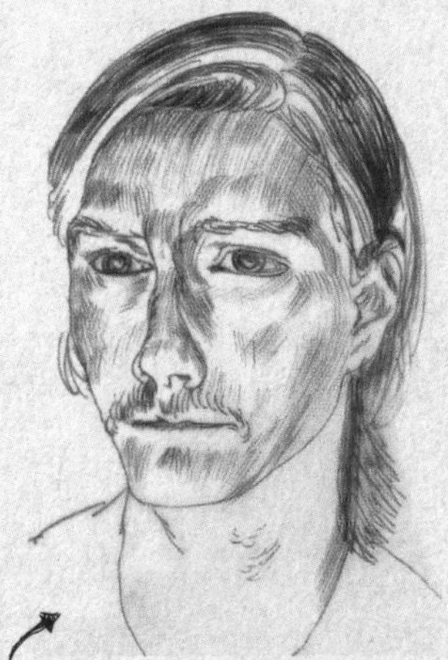

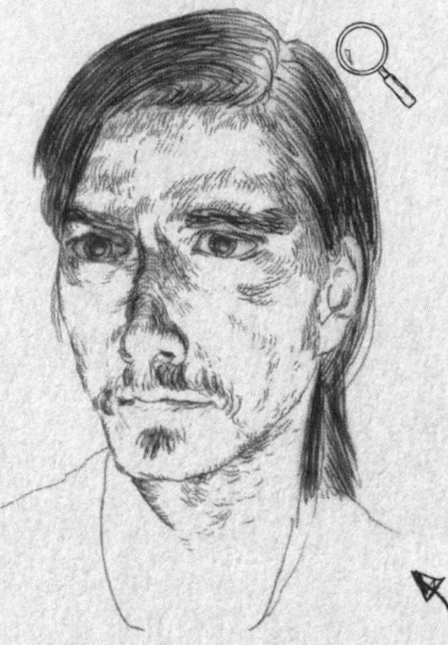

The same face—still lacking definition from an outline—has hatching moving across it both vertically and diagonally, giving it a more volumetric feel, as if it is emerging from the darkness. The crosshatch makes the face feel as though it is coming forward. The lines are describing the roundness of the face; it occupies a more three-dimensional reality and feels less ephemeral.

The same face, this time defined by an outline, is more structurally solid, but less dramatic. The outline fixes the head in space, making it feel sturdier and more stationary; there is less of a sense of motion. However, the figure feels stronger, not just graphically, but also psychologically; the mood is very different from the first two, even though they are drawn from the same reference. Each technique gives a different mood and personality to the figure: the first two are more mysterious and dramatic, and the third is more solid and confident.

The fourth example is drawn with an outline, and uses stippling instead of hatching, employing short dashes instead of long strokes. This creates a less fluid motion and is far more halting to the eye as it moves over the face, as if moving across a textural surface made up of small hairs or little bumps. This type of shading creates a more intense emotion, forces the eye of the viewer to focus more, and implies stress or anxiety along with awareness. Areas in this face that have a concentration of stippling become areas of the most intense focus. Building up stippling around the eyes generates greater attention, giving the subject a more thoughtful expression.

EXERCISE 2:

VOLUME WITH CROSSHATCHING

Ballpoint has a fairly fixed mark, without the variation in line weight a pencil or quill has. The evenness prevents a single line from conveying space or weight, which helps create the illusion of volume. To create volume with ballpoint, more detailed shading is necessary.

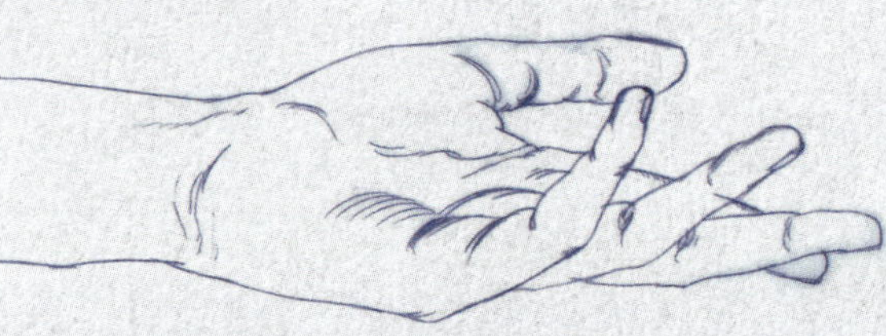

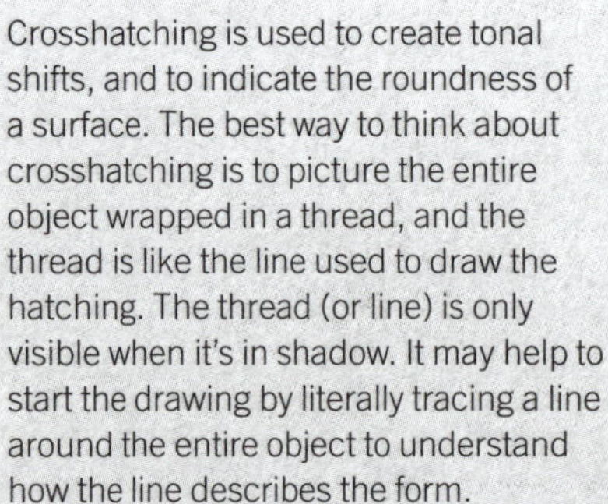

Crosshatching is used to create tonal shifts, and to indicate the roundness of a surface. The best way to think about crosshatching is to picture the entire object wrapped in a thread, and the thread is like the line used to draw the hatching. The thread (or line) is only visible when it's in shadow. It may help to start the drawing by literally tracing a line around the entire object to understand how the line describes the form.

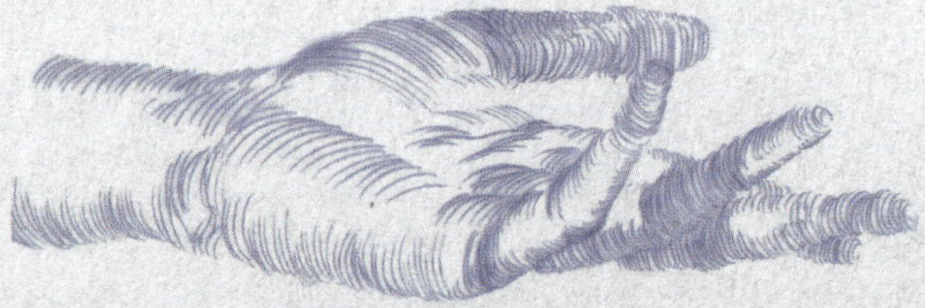

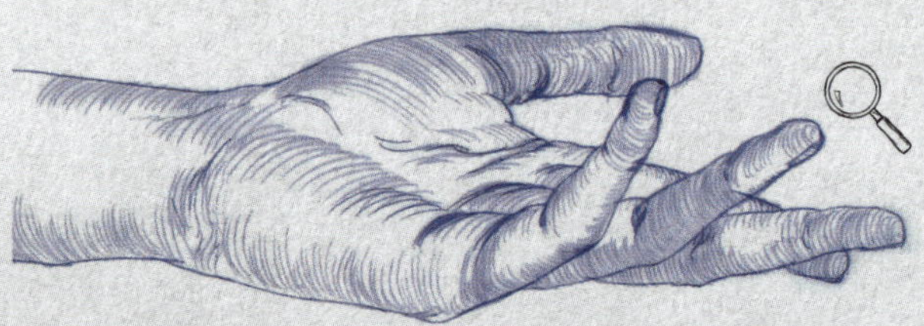

As the surface of a round object curves away in space (away from the viewer), the shadow will get darker; this is a gradated darkening. The gradation is achieved in two ways, by the lines converging, or by hatching lines on top of the first set.

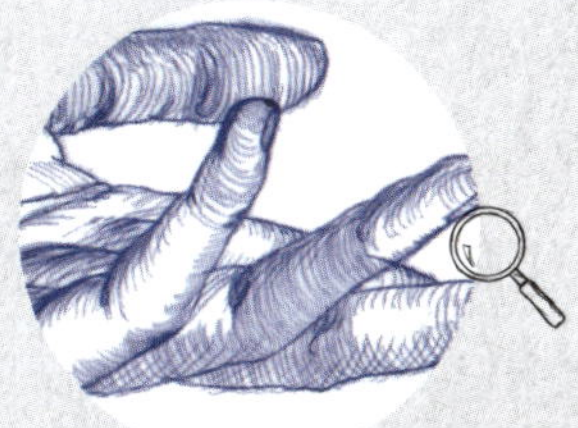

These lines cross over the lines underneath, thus the term *crosshatching*. The hatching of the lines can be nearly parallel (12 to 22 degrees) to give the shading a softer effect. Nearly perpendicular lines (up to 90 degrees in the hatching) give the shadow a sharper feeling and halt the flow of the lines.

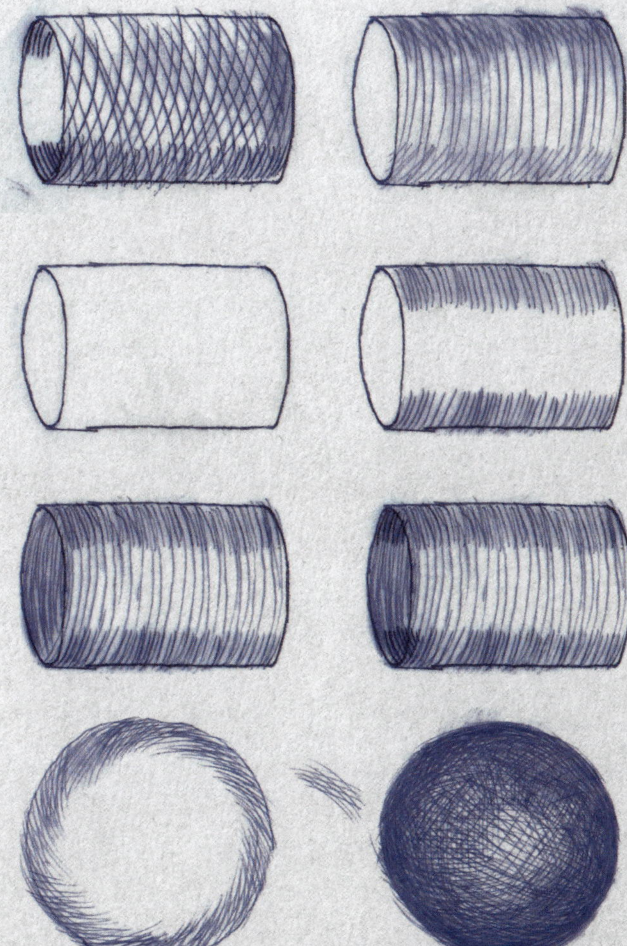

The lines can also be built up in more layers to create a fuller, or deeper, sense of space.

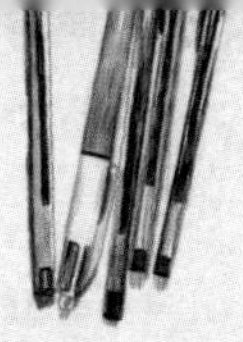

EXERCISE 3:

CREATING A LANDSCAPE WITH TEXTURE AND MARKS (BUT NO OUTLINES)

MARKS IN A DRAWING CAN BE ASSIGNED TO SPECIFIC SURFACES TO DESCRIBE THEM, WITHOUT LITERALLY DEPICTING THEM. A MARK IS AN ABSTRACT INDICATOR OF INFORMATION. IN THIS EXERCISE, THE DIFFERENT ELEMENTS ARE EACH ASSIGNED A SPECIFIC AND UNIQUE MARK. EACH MARK IS USED EXCLUSIVELY FOR THAT SURFACE OR OBJECT TO DESCRIBE THE SURFACE TONALLY.

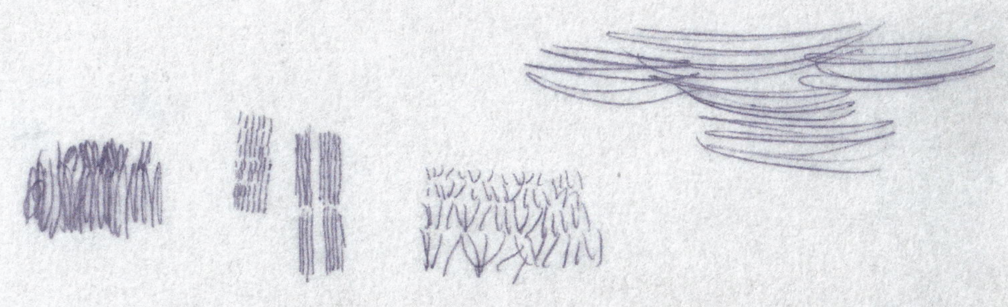

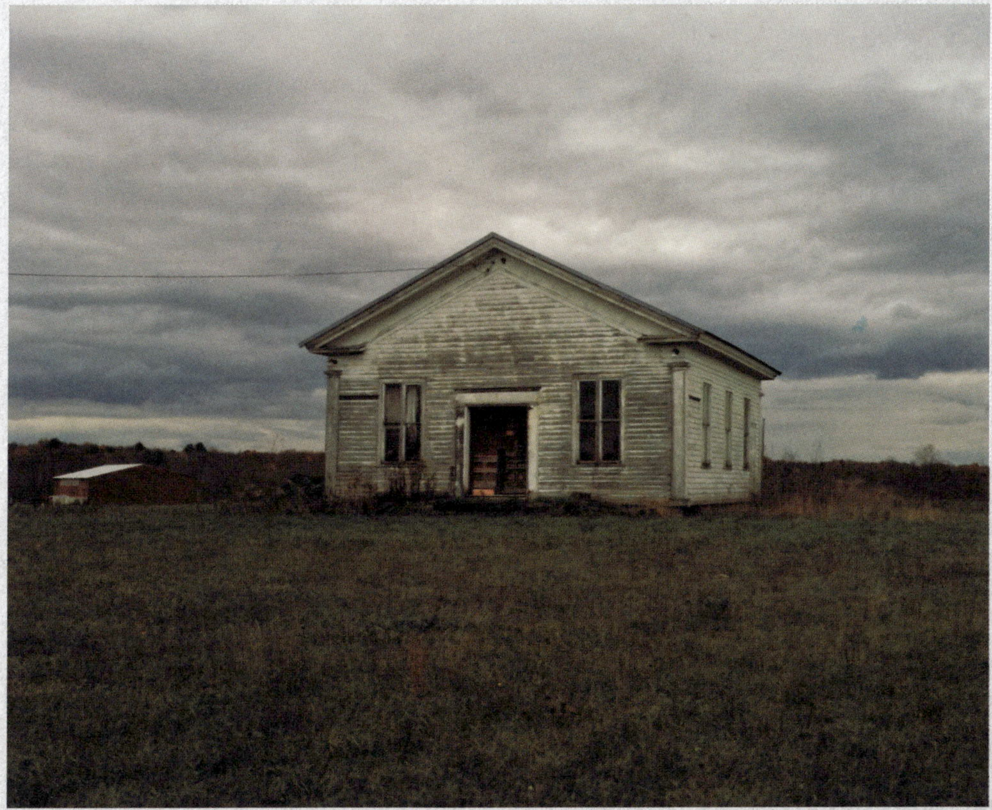

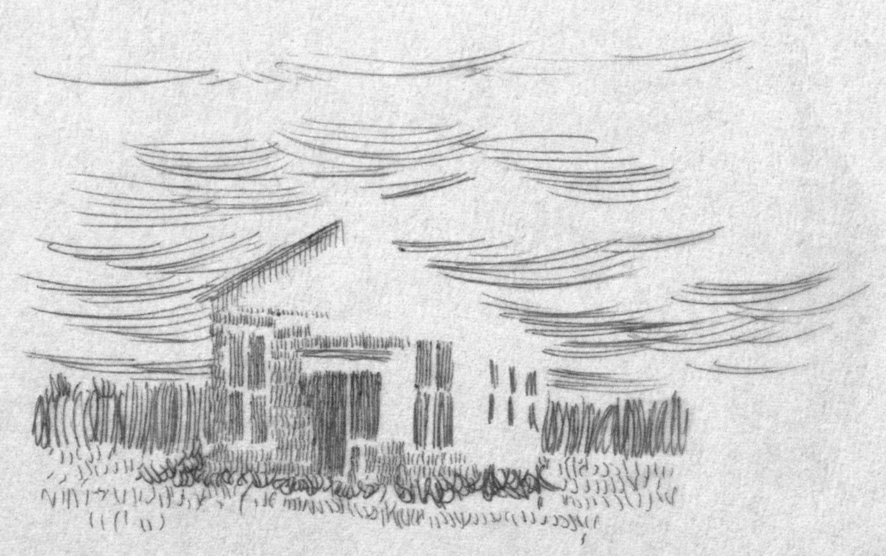

In this example, the grass is defined by a series of clustered dashes, usually three or more dashes at a time, and the dashes are curved slightly like blades of grass. They convey space as well as surface by diminishing in size as they are stacked on top of each other to give the impression of receding backward into the distance. The field of marks grows darker as it recedes, but also indicates a narrower range of contrast, whereas the marks closer to the bottom (and closer to the viewer illusionistically) are more spread out and longer. The field created is generally lighter as it gets closer in space, but also there is a wider range of contrast within the clusters of marks. The marks used to describe the walls of the building are dashes as well, but they are stacked uniformly and flatly.

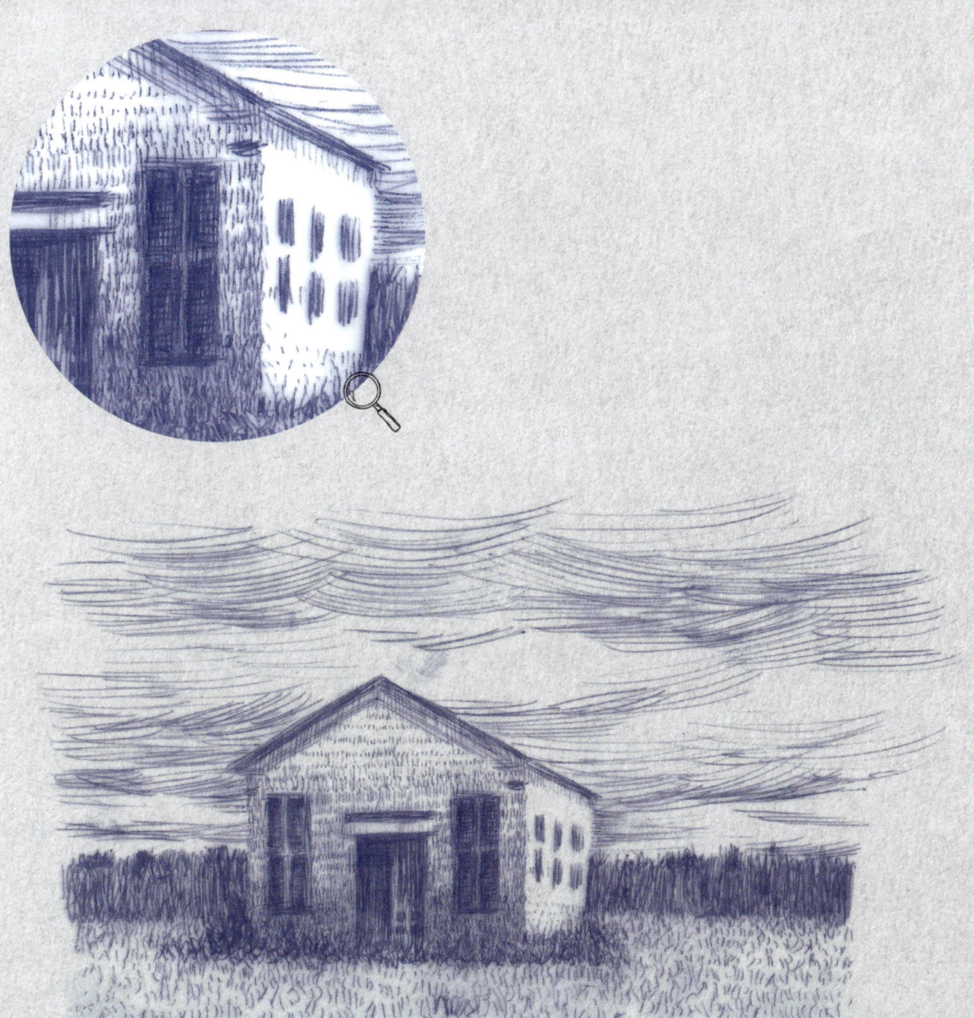

The marks are all even as they are stacked in rows on top of each other; this even stacking indicates a flat space, a wall that is not moving back in space. The space in between the dashes is filled in more tightly to add darkness to the shadows on the wall or spaced out more to create a sense of light.

The trees in the back are given long dashes, which prevent the detail from becoming as meticulous as in the wall or grass and helps push the trees further back in space. Similar to the grass, the long dashes have a curve to imply the organic nature of the trees. The windows are given similar long dashes, but as with the difference between the grass and the wood, the dashes for the window are straight and rigid to communicate a flat, manufactured surface. This difference between curved and straight lines prevents the two surfaces from becoming confused with each other.

The sky is described in long, horizontal strokes. The horizontal orientation relays the sense of motion of clouds moving across the sky and also creates a sharp contrast between objects on the ground, which all have marks moving vertically.

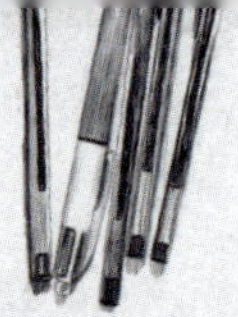

EXERCISE 4:

DRAWING ON TONED PAPER

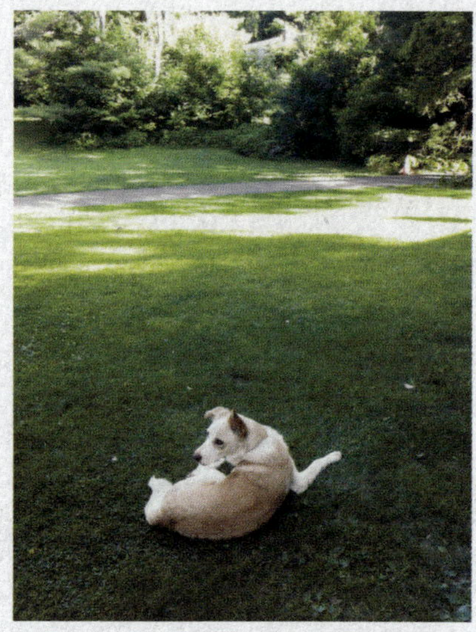

Using only ballpoint to describe the shadows and light in an image can lead to over-rendering an image, because fitting an entire range of value, lights, mid-tones, and shadows can be difficult to describe clearly. Working on a toned ground and using white acrylic can be a way to modulate the three values into manageable categories. Describing light in a drawing is a process of editing, because all of the information the eye sees cannot be relayed in the drawing. Thus, drawing tends to be a process of simplifying the details, say, in a shadow, down to manageable abstract shapes. Separating the three stages of value into three separate mediums simplifies the process, taking the burden off the pen to describe each clearly. In this process the stages of value are each assigned a medium, the darkest darks are delegated to the pen, the mid-tones to watercolor, and the highlights to acrylic.

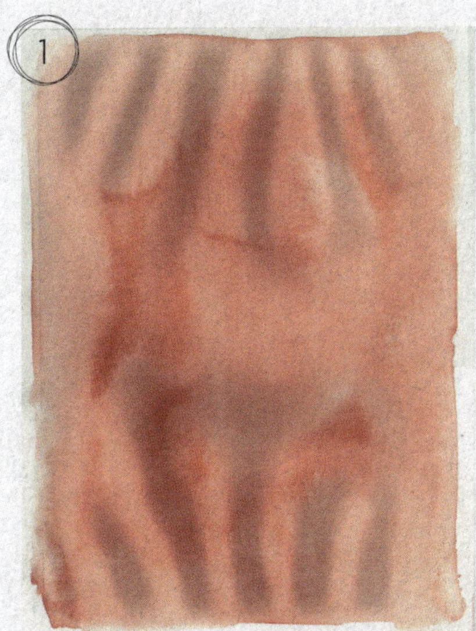

The first step of the process is to tone a sheet of paper before doing any drawing. To achieve an even tone, mix enough watercolor to create a wash over the entire paper. You can prepare this on a watercolor palette or in a small cup, and then with a large, clean brush, spread a single wash of clean water over the page. Then, while the page is still wet, apply the watercolor. This wet-on-wet technique will spread the watercolor evenly across the page with no brushstrokes visible. Let the page dry completely. At this point, it is okay to lightly sketch in the composition with pencil. (If the drawing is done lightly, the pencil is easily erased later; if the pencil is overworked, it will leave a texture on the page that will make the ballpoint stage of the drawing more difficult.) It is good at this stage to also indicate where the highlights will be painted in.

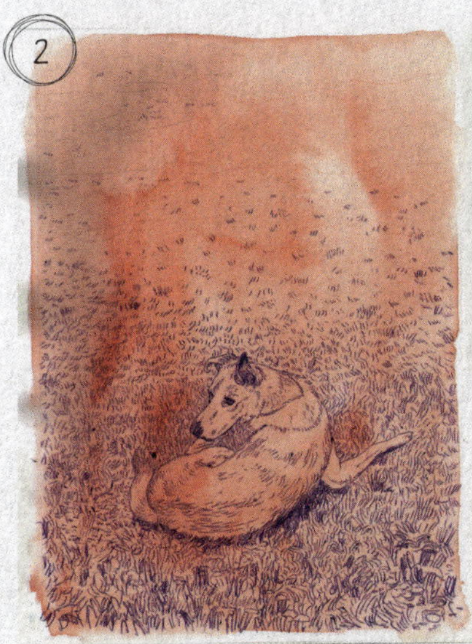

The next step is to begin drawing with ballpoint. The ballpoint's purpose here is to only capture the darkest darks, the shadows and outlines of objects, so this will be a somewhat simpler application of ballpoint than if there were no tone, as the watercolor is doing the job of occupying the middle ground.

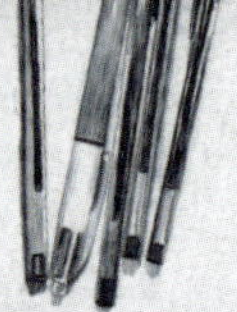

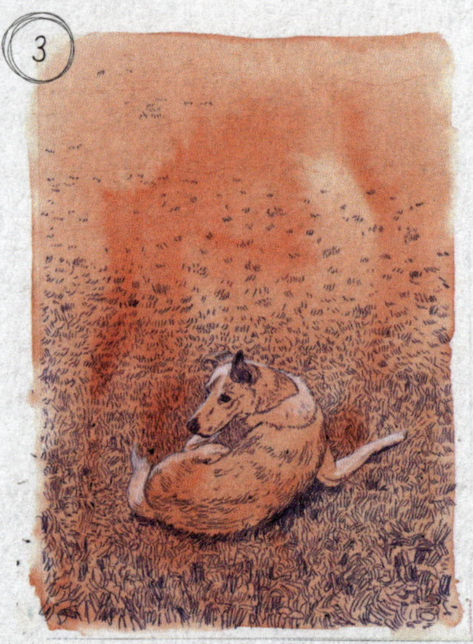

Once the ballpoint is complete (it may be best to stop before the drawing looks done: understate the ballpoint, and don't fuss too much at this point), apply the acrylic in two stages. The first is as a wash that is transparent. Water down the white acrylic so that it is not completely opaque, and draw in the highlights with a brush like a watercolor wash. The wetness will activate the watercolor underneath the acrylic, blending the two and creating not a true white, but a lighter version of the wash. When drawing in the highlights with the brush, it is important to follow the same sort of texture and mark making that was done with the pen. Apply areas of detail with a fine-tipped brush, so that the same marks achieved with the ballpoint can be mimicked with the brush.

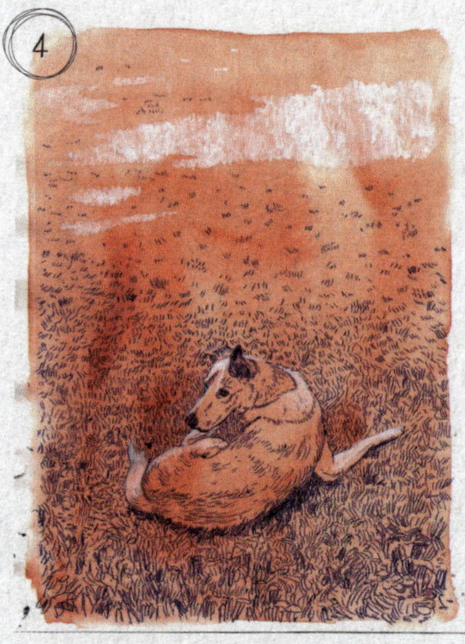

Once this dries, look back at the reference, and identify a smaller portion of the highlights that are the brightest of the highlights. To this more narrow range of white, apply the acrylic opaquely. The acrylic should not be watered down or transparent, but totally opaque, and it should not be applied over all of the transparent wash of acrylic, only the brightest sections.

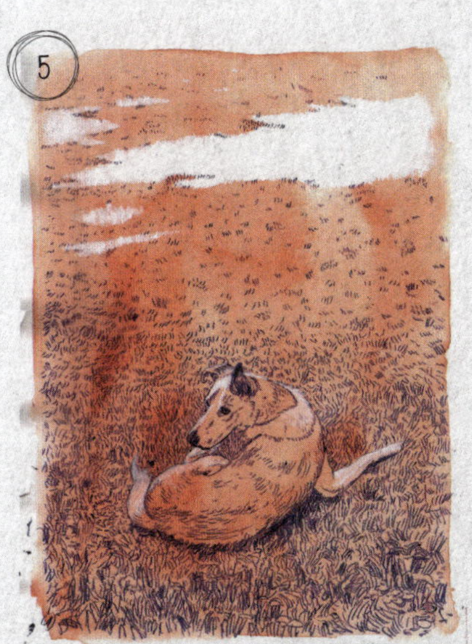

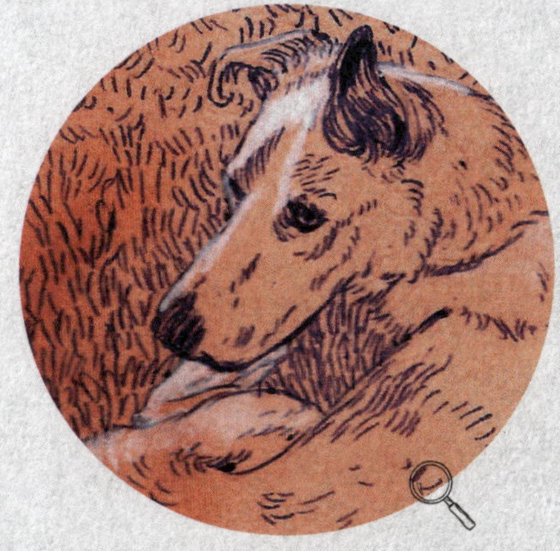

In the end this should leave four variations of tone, the darkest in ballpoint, the middle in watercolor, and two stages of highlight—the transparent wash of acrylic and the opaque.

GALLERY: CONTEMPORARY CLASSICAL

FEATURED ARTIST:

DINA BRODSKY

Dina Brodsky is primarily a painter, though drawing, particularly in her sketchbooks, is an integral part of her creative process, akin to a visual diary. Drawing in them is a necessity, like eating and sleeping. She's had a sketchbook in her bag every day for the past fifteen years or so. It's only in ballpoint, and she carries it everywhere. Because Dina is primarily a painter, her sketchbooks become more about play, or research, or just fun, the thing she gets to experiment with when not working on more finished oil paintings. Every once in a while she will use her sketchbook drawings as preparatory sketches for more finished work, but most of the time they don't make it out of the sketchbook, or if they do it's not until years later.

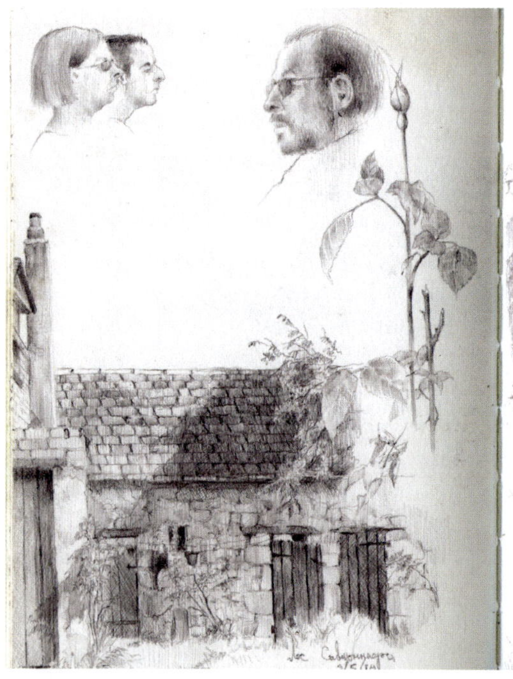

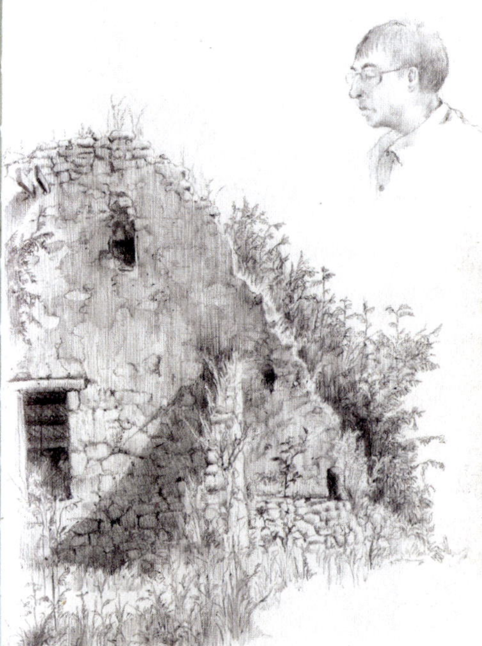

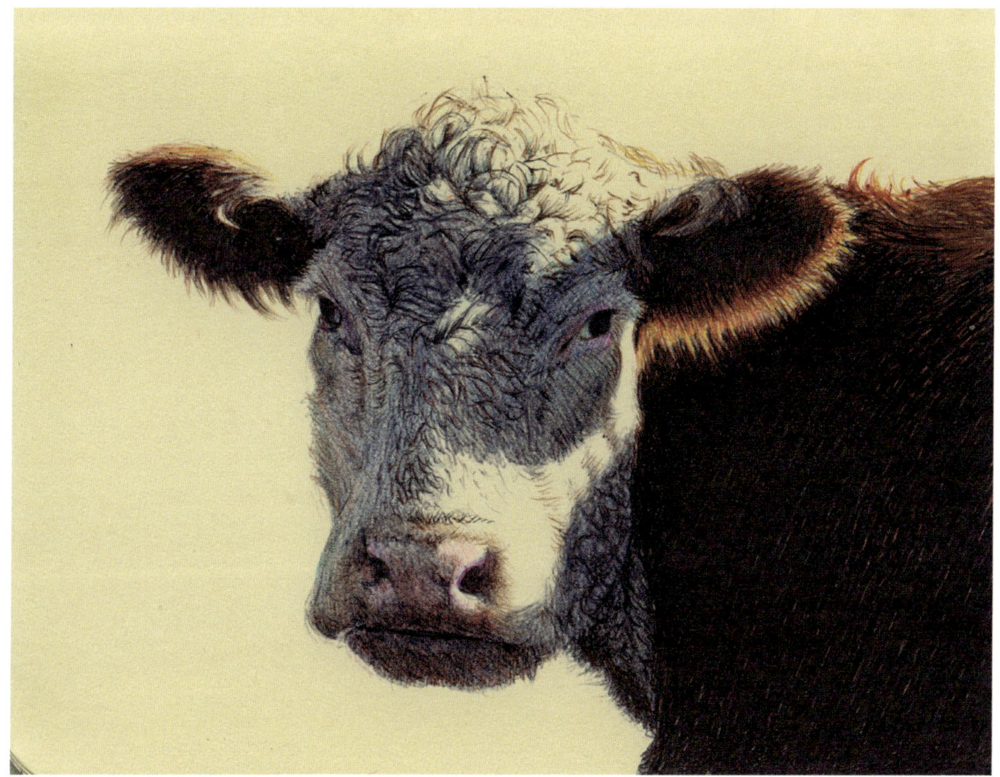

The Claim 1
(excerpt), 2012
Colored ballpoint pen
3½ x 5½ inches
(9 x 14 cm)

FEATURED ARTIST:

NICOLAS V. SANCHEZ

Nicolas Sanchez began drawing in black ink at his leisure while attending graduate school at the New York Academy of Art. Assignments and studio time were demanding, so drawing in a sketchbook on the subway or on a plane was a way to release that pressure and create something that was not meant to be exhibited. It allowed for a healthy stream of consciousness.

For Nicolas, ballpoint pen offers a sense of freedom. There is no preliminary pencil drawing. He starts with the pen and just continues drawing. "There's no taking it back," he says, "so why worry about it? It pushes me to become more disciplined and develop a sense of agility when working with ink." He also works more quickly in ink, finishing a drawing much faster than work in graphite or oil paint because of its permanent quality.

Image Highlights:

Guno Park
Chimpanzee, 2014
Ink on paper
7 x 11 inches
(18 x 28 cm)

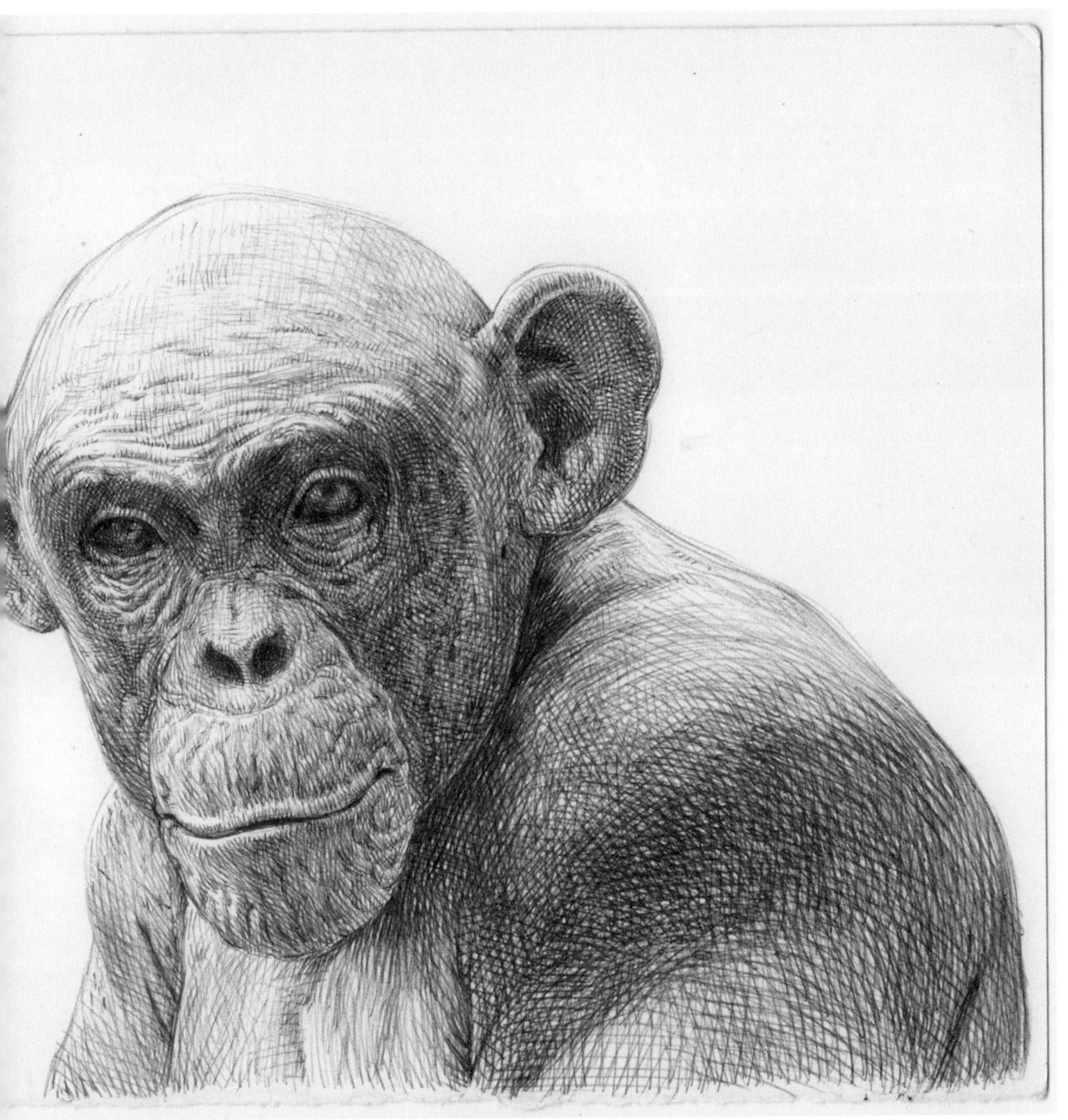

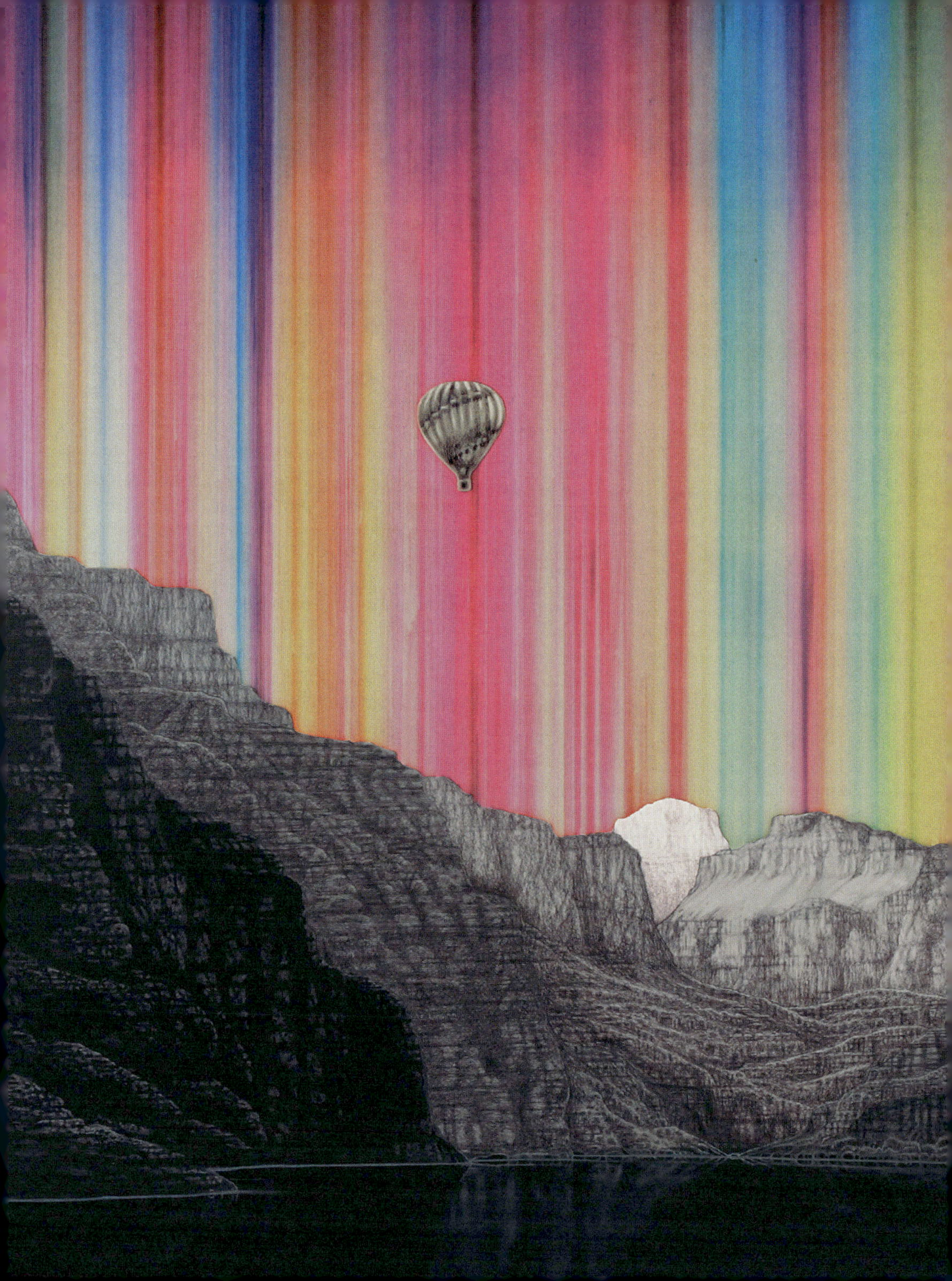

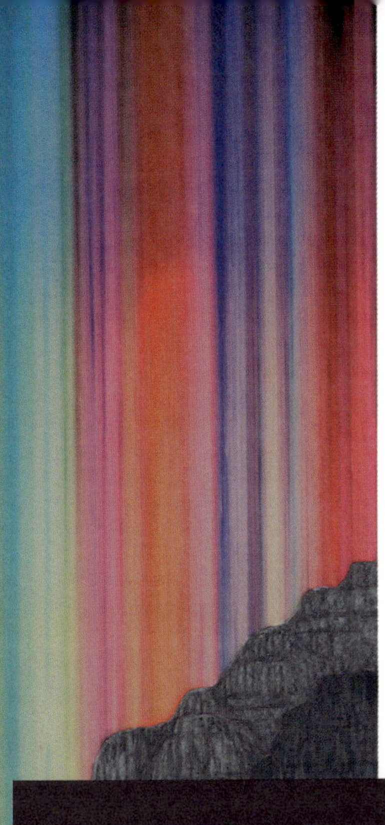

Shane McAdams
Hot Air, 2013
Ballpoint pen, oil, and resin on panel
48 x 48 inches
(122 x 122 cm)

CHAPTER 2: CONTEMPORARY ABSTRACTION

The exercises featured in this chapter explore the limitations and very nature of the pen. The techniques stem from unique qualities found in ballpoint. In these processes, the medium can become the subject itself or in some way is integral to the overall concept of the design. The limitations and nature of ballpoint make these abstractions possible.

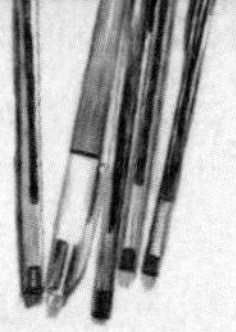

EXERCISE 5:

CREATING AN EVEN FIELD OF MARKS

TO CREATE A FIELD OF MARKS (NOT A REPEATING PATTERN SO MUCH AS A CLOUD), FIRST DECIDE ON A TYPE OF MARK. IN THIS INSTANCE, THE MARKS ARE SMALL DASHES AND LONG STROKES.

With either of these marks, start by creating a small cluster, not too dense, and far enough apart to be able to fill more of the marks in between the initial ones applied. This is a microcosm of the rest to the field.

Expand further out from here. Do not work or linger too long on any area; move around the page so that the marks are being applied evenly. Loosely expand the marks to the edge of the areas that make up the field. At this point, the area of the field should be defined, but the interior will look like little islands of marks with open spaces in between them. The islands of marks should be somewhat evenly spaced. The rest of the process is like a game, and the goal of the game is to fill in the empty spaces, but again, not lingering in one area too long, or else the field will be uneven. Move briskly around the page, filling in the empty spaces.

It helps to squint at the field. Squinting will blur the marks into a foggy tone and reveal where the largest open areas remain. The idea is to always move to the most open area and fill it with marks until it is even with the rest of the tone and then move on to the next most open area. Slowly, the fields will look less like isolated islands and will congeal together into an even tone. As the spaces in between each cluster grow smaller, the clusters of marks filled in between these spaces should also grow smaller, until it is only one mark at a time that is being applied.

Always looking for the lightest area to add marks, continue to fill the gaps until the field is as dark as desired.

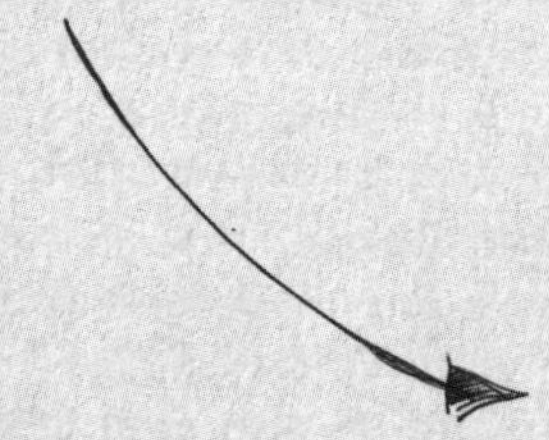

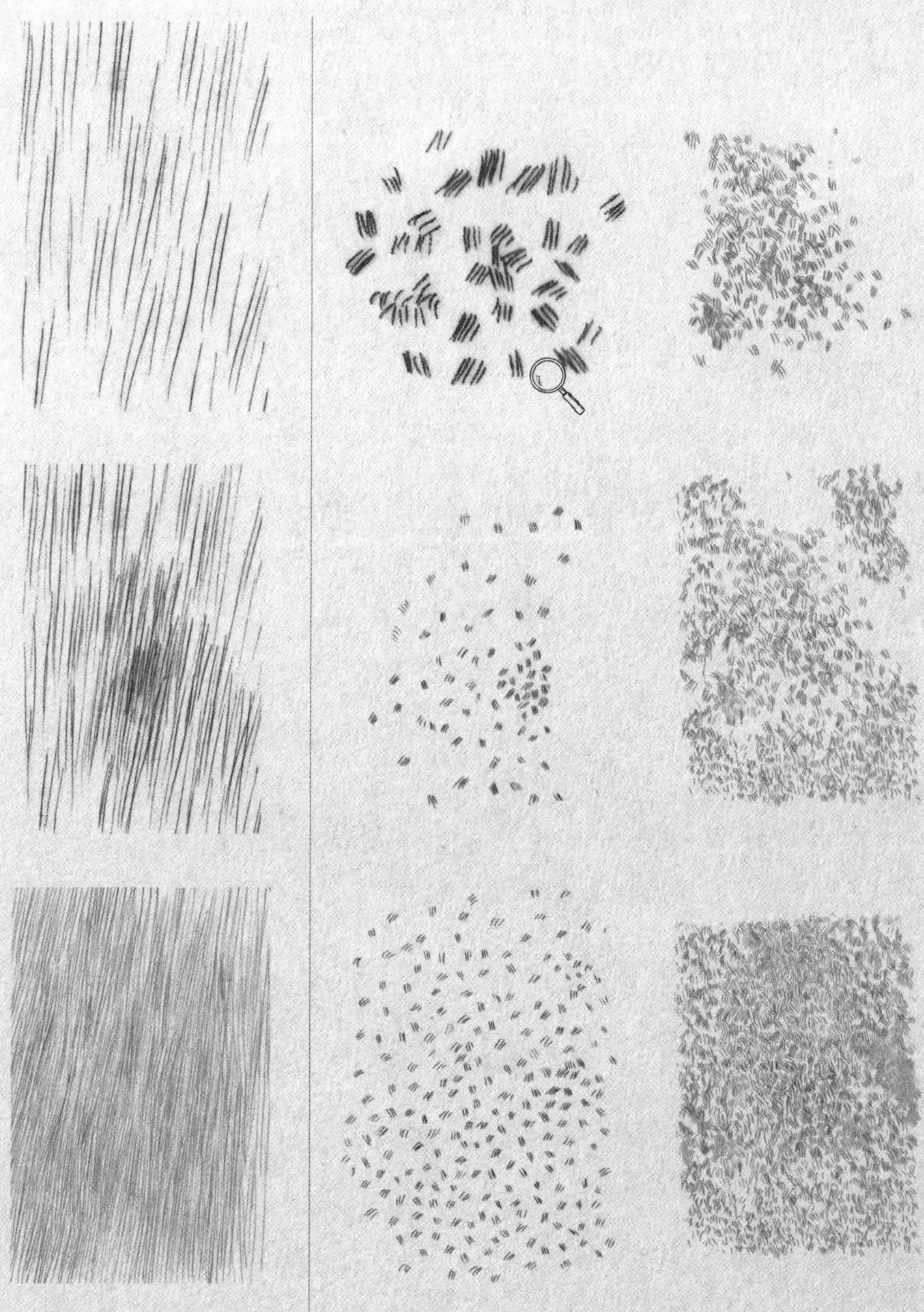

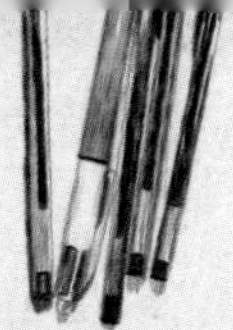

EXERCISE 6:

SCRIBBLE

THE IDEA OF THIS ASSIGNMENT IS NOT TO THINK, BUT DRAW. LET THE MOTION OF THE WRIST CREATE THE MARKS IN A FREE-FLOWING MANNER. THE FIRST STEP IS TO FREE THE MIND FROM WORRY ABOUT MAKING A "BAD DRAWING." IT FREES THE ARTIST OF THE IDEA THAT A DRAWING IS A "PRECIOUS" THING, AND ALLOWING THE MARK TO LEAD THE DRAWING, AND THE MOTION OF THE WRIST OR ARM TO CONTROL THE MARK, ACCOMPLISHES THIS.

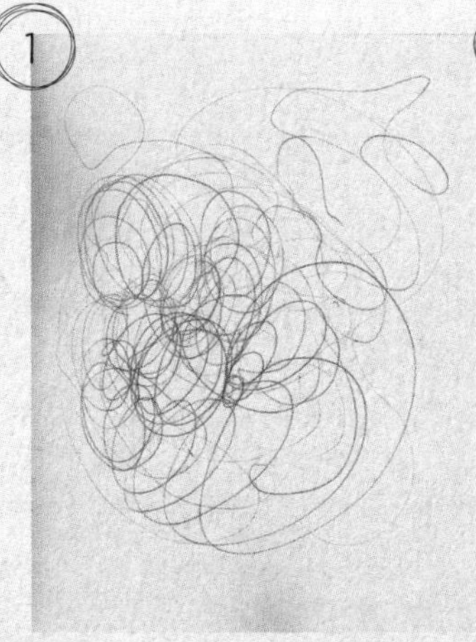

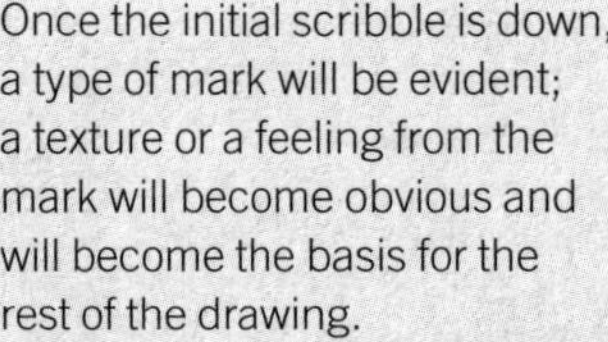
Once the initial scribble is down, a type of mark will be evident; a texture or a feeling from the mark will become obvious and will become the basis for the rest of the drawing.

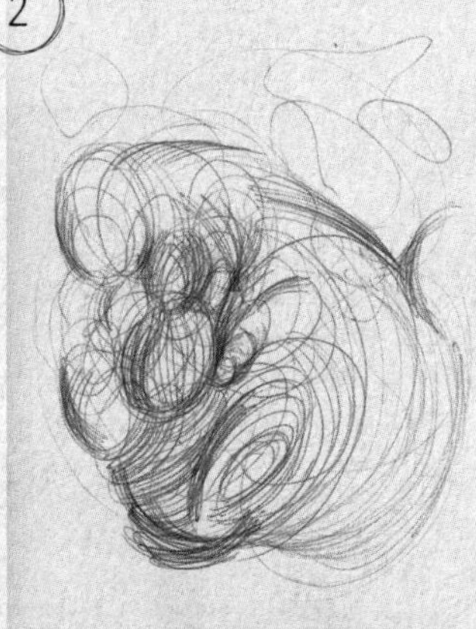

Begin to build the drawing up following the initial marks and begin to look for a form. This does not need to be a three-dimensional form, but more a point of interest.

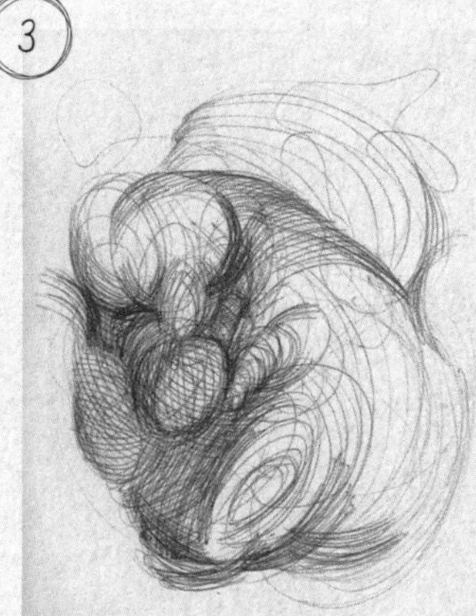

The drawing may become a bit of a mess, so once this point is reached, try to define the parts of interest with more clarity. Refine and define these parts. Do not be afraid of overdrawing, as this is really just a sketch.

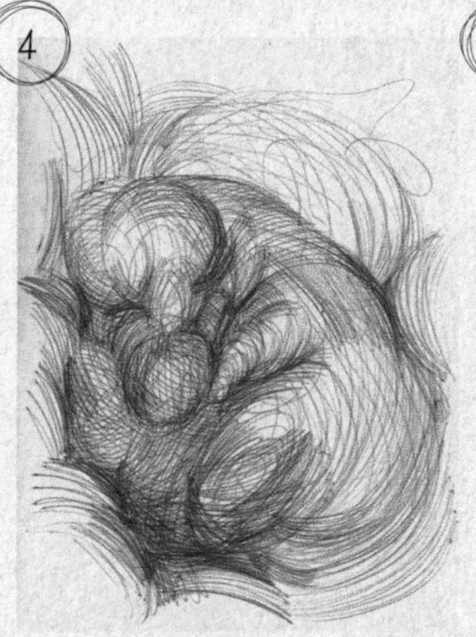

This drawing should be pushed further than is comfortable. If the drawing looks finished, continue to work. Go beyond what is comfortable, or "pretty"; this will possibly ruin the drawing, but it will also help reveal new possibilities. It will also stretch the concept of what "done" means in a drawing and allow for more confidence in subsequent drawings.

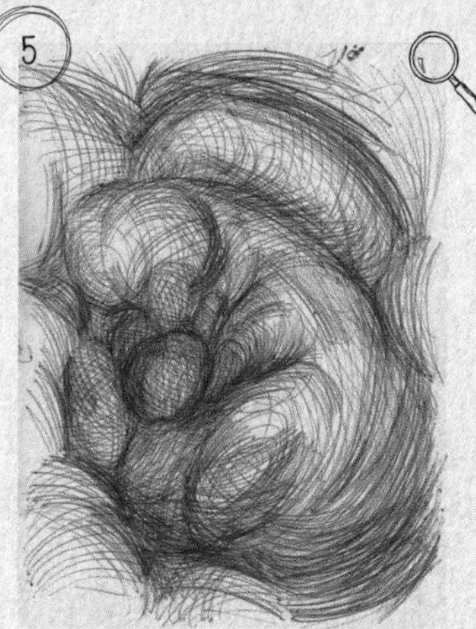

This is a practice that should be repeated multiple times, and quickly without thinking too much about it. Try it at least four times in one sitting. By the last drawing, there will be a certain abandon in the process, a looseness and confidence, as any anxiety about messing up the drawing will be overcome. This looseness is not something applied only to abstract scribbles in a sketchbook, but also helps in representational drawing and drawing from life. It will do two things: help with understanding how far a drawing can go before it is overworked and alleviate the fear of mark making. This is particularly useful with ballpoint because it cannot be erased, and the marks laid out on the page are permanent.

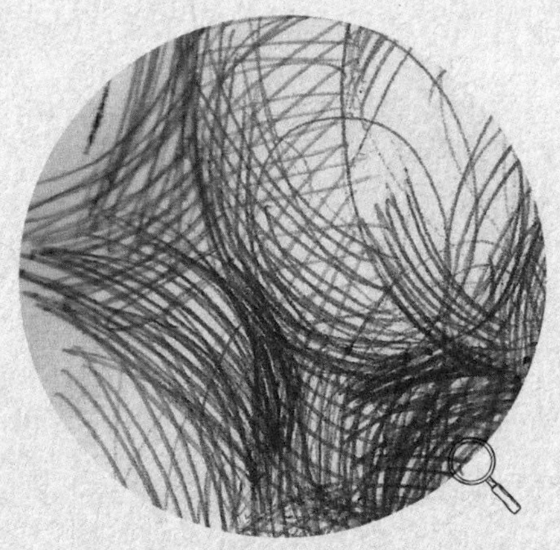

EXERCISE 7:

RESPONDING TO AN ORGANIC PROCESS

THE OBJECT OF THIS EXERCISE IS TO CREATE A NATURAL PROCESS, TO USE A MEDIUM IN A WAY THAT IS NOT TYPICAL DRAWING, BUT A DRAWING THAT IS DICTATED BY THE NATURE OF THE MEDIUM (IN THIS CASE, FROZEN WATERCOLOR). THE PROCESS IS ORGANIC AND WILL CREATE A NATURAL AND UNPLANNED COMPOSITION THAT RELATES TO THE NATURE OF THE MATERIAL. THIS IS MEANT TO TAKE THE CONTROL OF THE COMPOSITION OUT OF THE ARTIST'S HANDS, FORCING A RESPONSE TO THE PROCESS. LOSS OF CONTROL IS A KEY ELEMENT TO THIS EXERCISE.

In this particular process, the goal is to create a stain out of a watercolor wash. The stain is the outcome of frozen watercolor thawing on a piece of paper.

Mix watercolor, put it in an ice cube tray, and freeze it. Place the frozen ice cube on a sheet of paper; as the ice melts, the pigment spreads across the page. The wetness will cause the paper to buckle and warp, channeling the paint according to the bending of the paper. This creates a natural mark, something like a wash or brushstroke, but not created by a human hand. The process of thawing allows the watercolor to create its own lines, seen as ripples within the shape of the wash. These are like layers of a wash created by an artist, but the intention is random and without purpose.

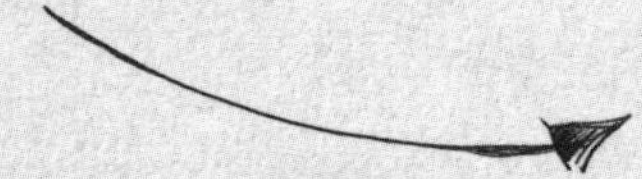

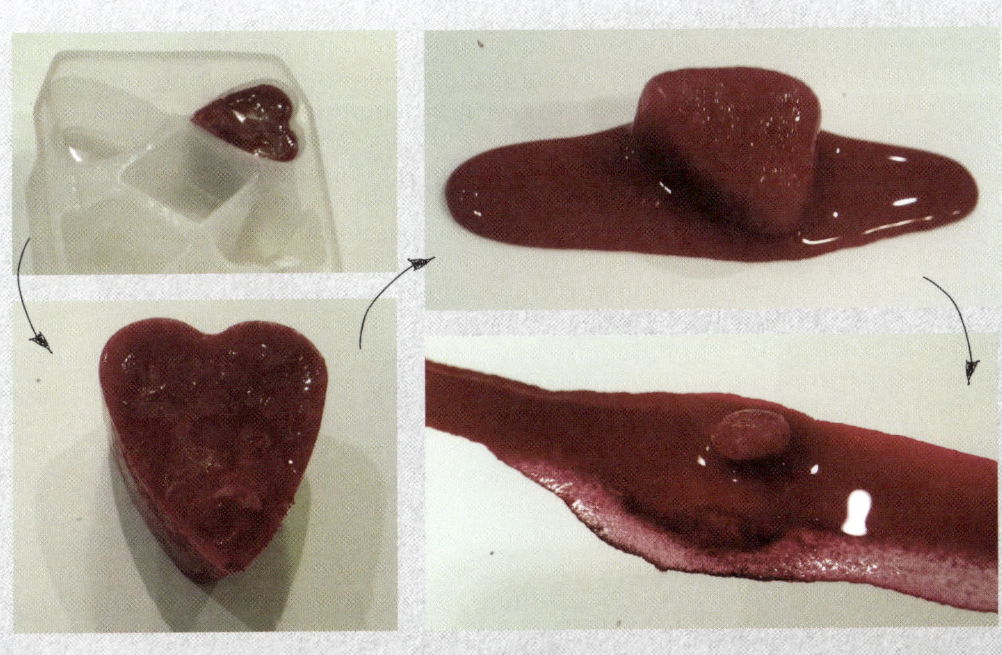

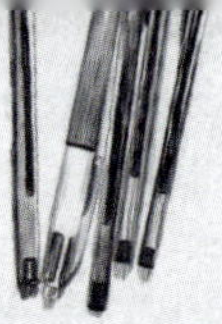

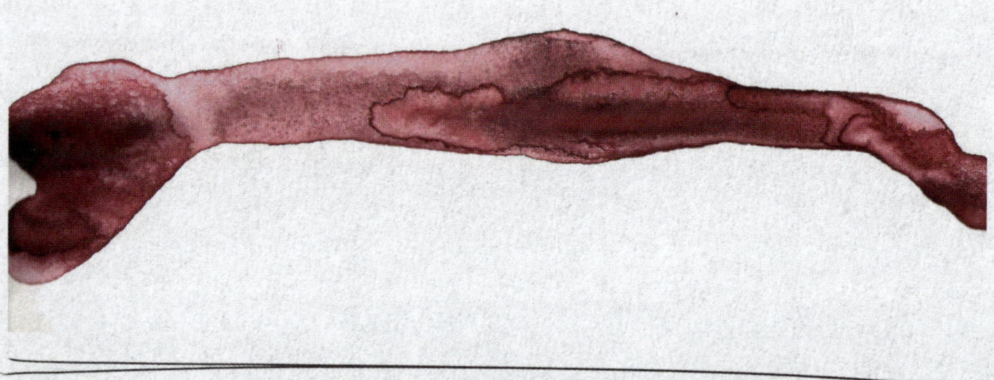

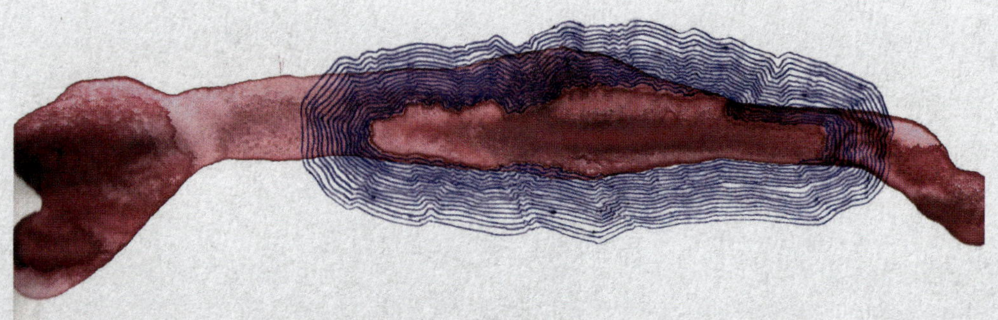

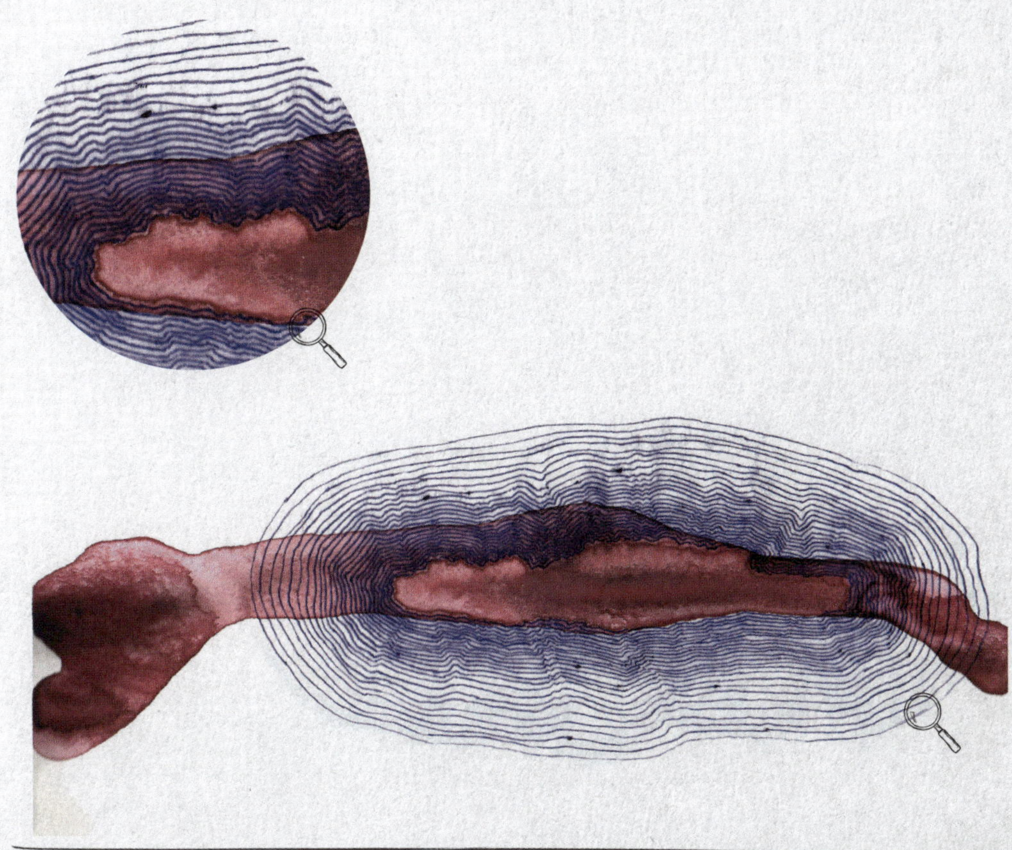

Once the wash dries, the organic layers of paint left behind create a sort of drawing, where lines are visible. These "lines" become the basis for the rest of the drawing. The process here is to find these lines and continue them. In this case, ballpoint is used to trace these lines and continue the act of rippling outward, mimicking the natural process. That is the only intent: simply continue to repeat and expand the "drawing" left by the ice.

These new lines created by the artist will inevitably take on a life of their own. Use the lines of the watercolor as the basis but allow the new drawn lines to evolve as well. The process here should be to simply repeat in a meditative act the lines in a concentric circle from the wash and allow the ballpoint lines to evolve, mirroring the nature of melted paint, but also reflecting the hand of the artist.

By leaving the rules simple, the drawing of the artist itself reflects the natural process of transformation of ice into water. The lines will evolve from a random state created by nature into an organized state created by a human. This reflects the act of order dissolving into random chaos and then back again into a controlled order.

GALLERY: CONTEMPORARY ABSTRACTION

FEATURED ARTIST:

JOAN SALÓ

Joan Saló's work involves creating a harmony of straight lines using a full spectrum of colored pens. In Joan's work, his materials and technique reflect the concept, which drives the piece. His drawings can be seen as large expressionistic works, and his process is engineered to express a clean, pure, uninhibited form of emotion.

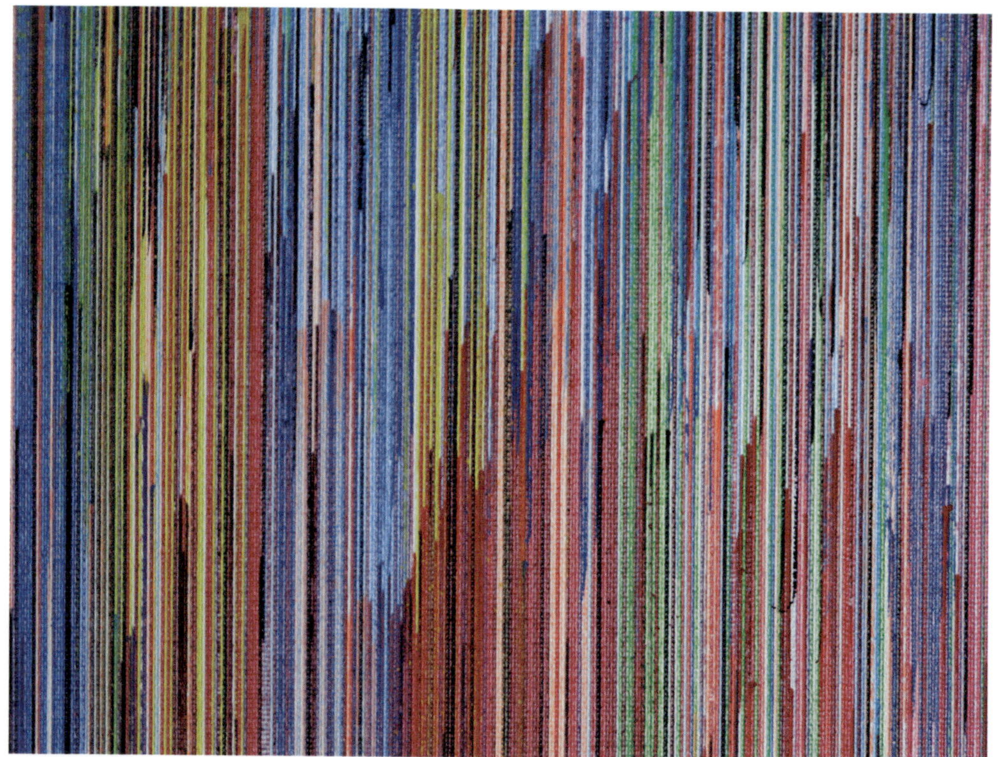

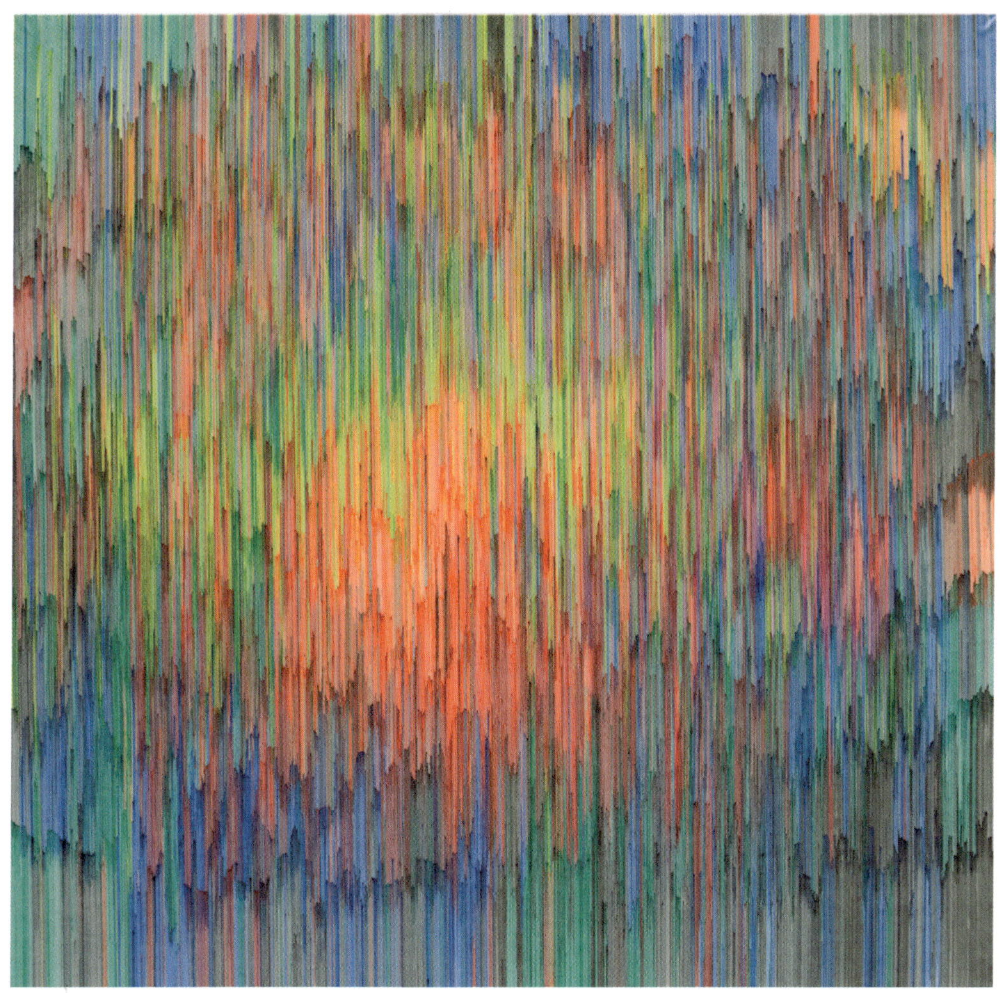

Opposite:
Untitled,
detail, 2014
Ballpoint pen
on canvas
79 x 79 inches
(200 x 200 cm)

Above:
Untitled, 2010
Ballpoint pen
on canvas
79 x 79 inches
(200 x 200 cm)

The straight line removes his gesture, and personality, from the mark. The repeating and layering of nondescript straight lines, a practice that consciously evokes Tibetan mandala making, creates a meditative process, a sensation that can also be invoked in the viewer.

Right:
Untitled, 2003
Ballpoint
12 x 12 inches
(30.5 x 30.5 cm)

Below:
Untitled, 2008
Ballpoint
12 x 12 inches
(30.5 x 30.5 cm)

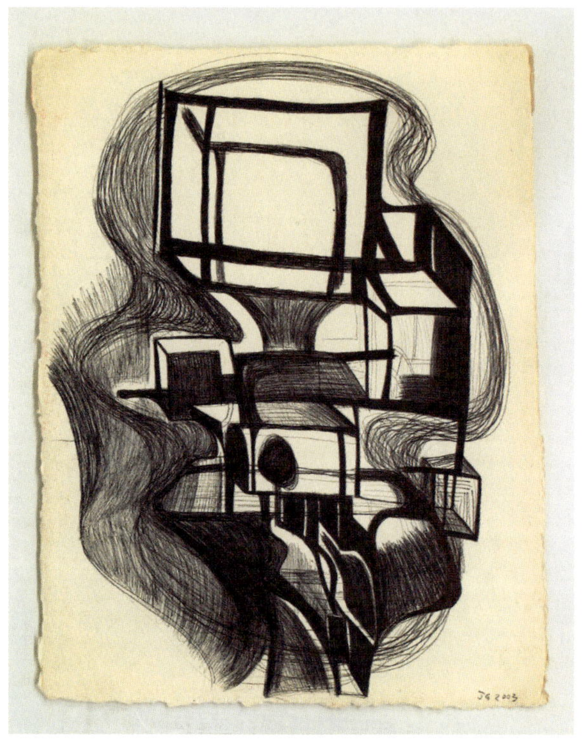

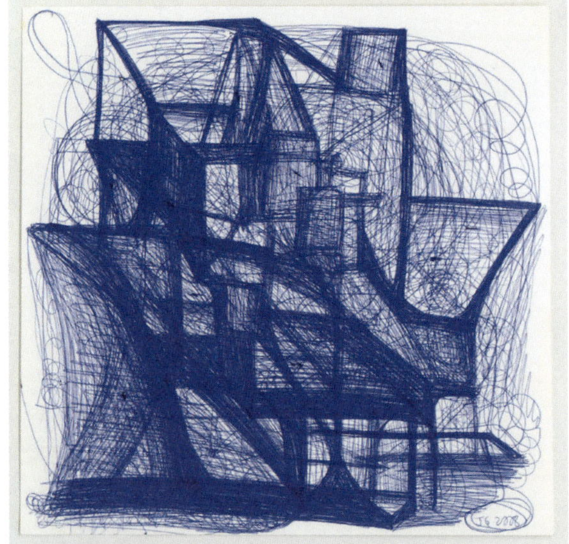

FEATURED ARTIST:

JOANNE GREENBAUM

Joanne Greenbaum's drawings just begin. When she's drawing, she starts by picking up the pen and seeing what happens, with no goal in mind. She sometimes sits and just scribbles; other times, it's something more detailed and analytical. The forms emerge as she draws. The forms she creates come from a pictorial language that interests her, mostly a fictional architecture that acts as a scaffolding to make impossible spaces. It is important to look at the drawings as forms and structures, not specific or in any way referring to the real world. The dimensions and geometry are imaginary, psychological.

FEATURED ARTIST:

SHANE MCADAMS

Shane's paintings capture a balance between realistic depictions of landscapes combined with process-based abstractions, though the abstractions themselves seem to imply a space similar to a landscape.

Below:
Pen Blow 66, 2011
Ballpoint pen and resin on panel
12 x 12 inches
(30.5 x 30.5 cm)

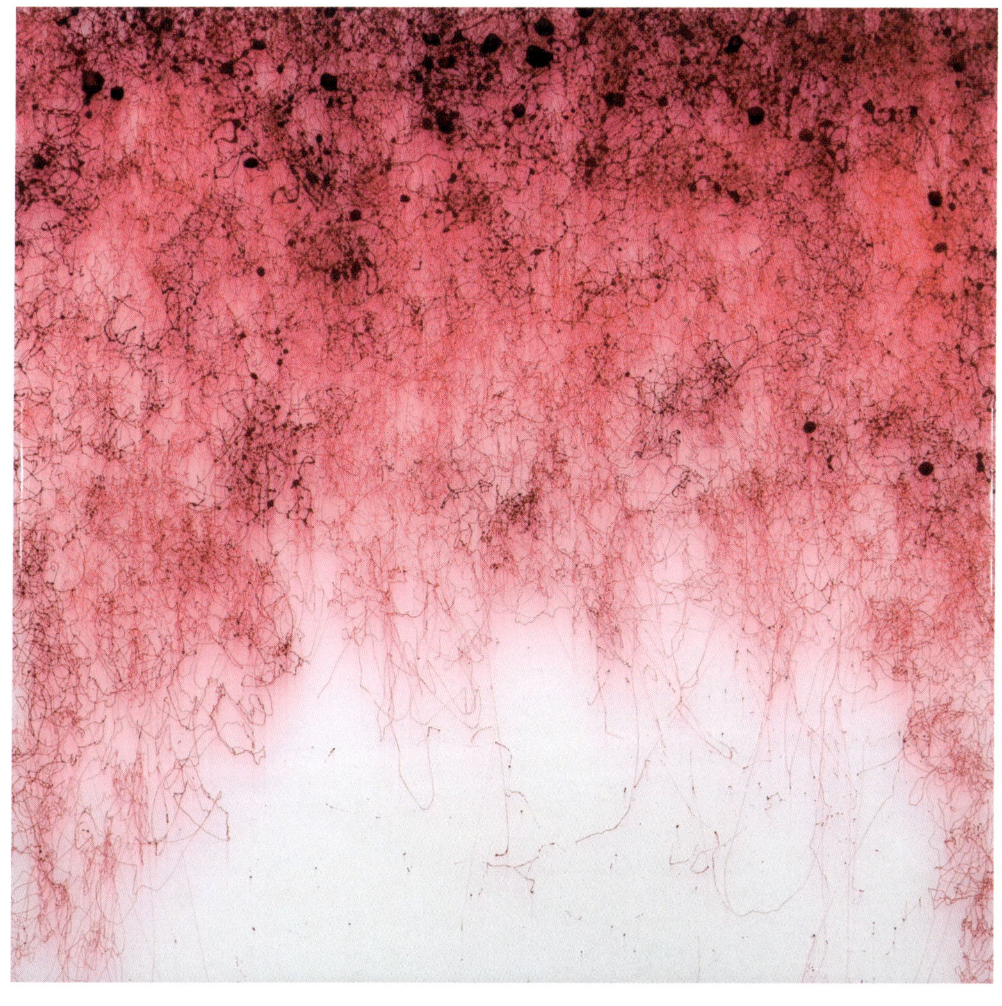

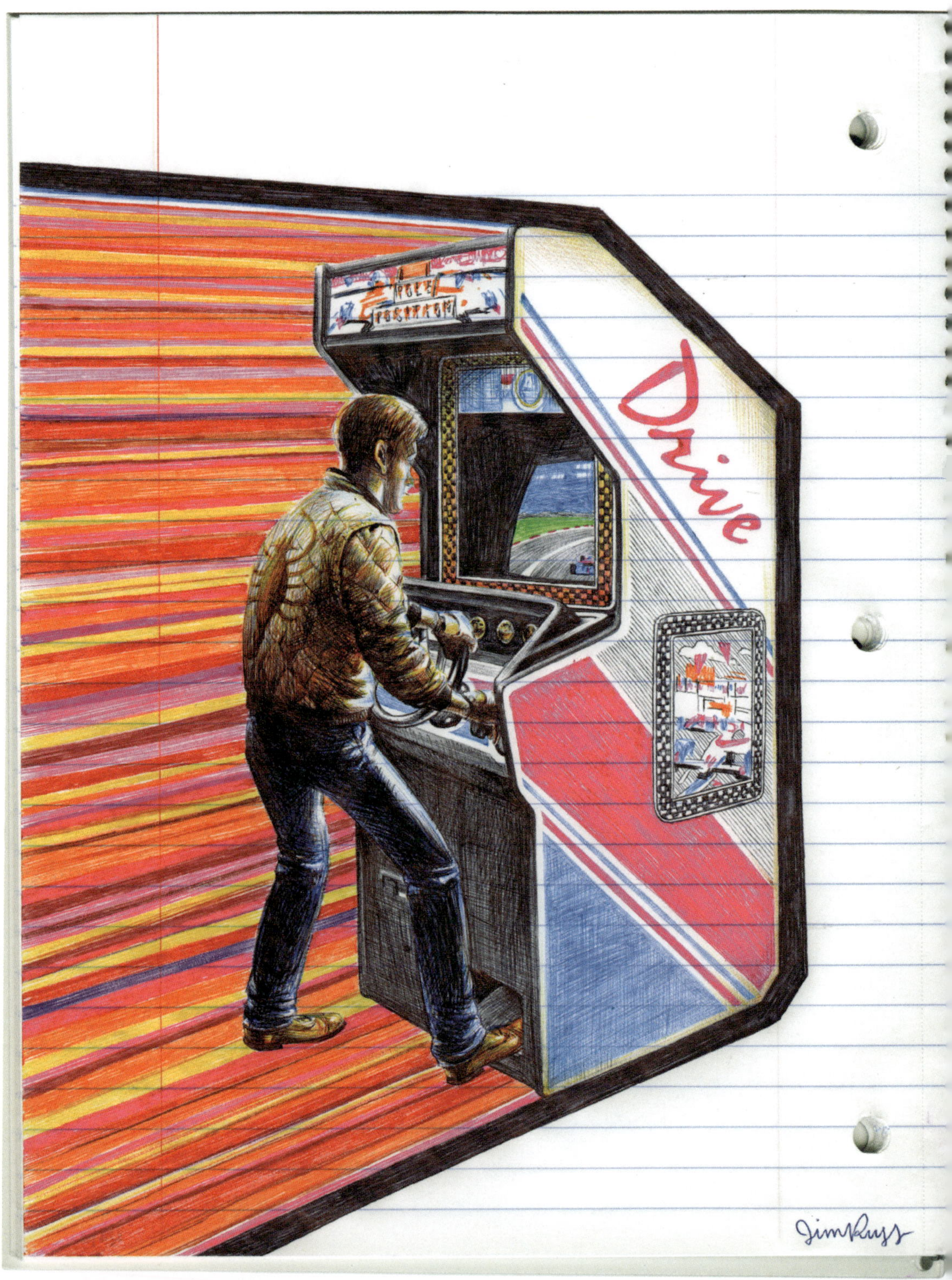
POLE
POSITION
Drive

Jim Rugg
Drive, 2012
Ballpoint pen on paper
8½ x 11 inches
(21.6 x 28 cm)

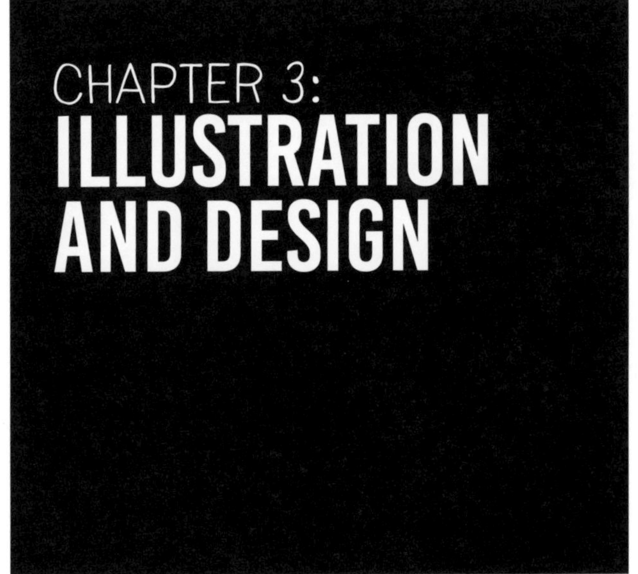

CHAPTER 3: ILLUSTRATION AND DESIGN

In this chapter the ballpoint pen is used as a graphic tool: its fixed line weight and consistent line quality make for an easily reproducible (mass-produced) format. The exercises are much more abstract, dealing with patterns and design elements rather than drafting and rendering of form. The unique quality of the ballpoint pen allows it to be both delicate and bold, but always a tool of precision and clarity, properties that are also highlighted by the gallery artists in this chapter.

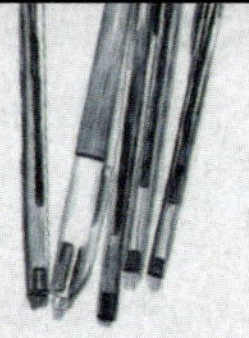

EXERCISE 8:

BLENDING COLOR

BLENDING COLORS WITH BALLPOINT IS A PROCESS OF LAYERING BY WAY OF CROSSHATCHING THE COLORS OF THE PEN. THE COLORS THAT COME DIRECTLY FROM THE PEN TEND TO BE BOLD, AND THE SPECTRUM IS REPRESENTED MAINLY WITH PRIMARY AND SECONDARY COLORS: RED, YELLOW, BLUE, GREEN, ORANGE, PURPLE, PINK, AND BROWN. THE BLUES, REDS, AND GREENS TEND TO HAVE LIGHTER AND DARKER VERSIONS THAT CAN BE USEFUL FOR SHADING, BUT THIS IS A LIMITED RANGE COMPARED WITH THE COLOR RANGE OF, SAY, A 500-COLOR PENCIL COLLECTION OR A 200-COLOR PASTEL SET.

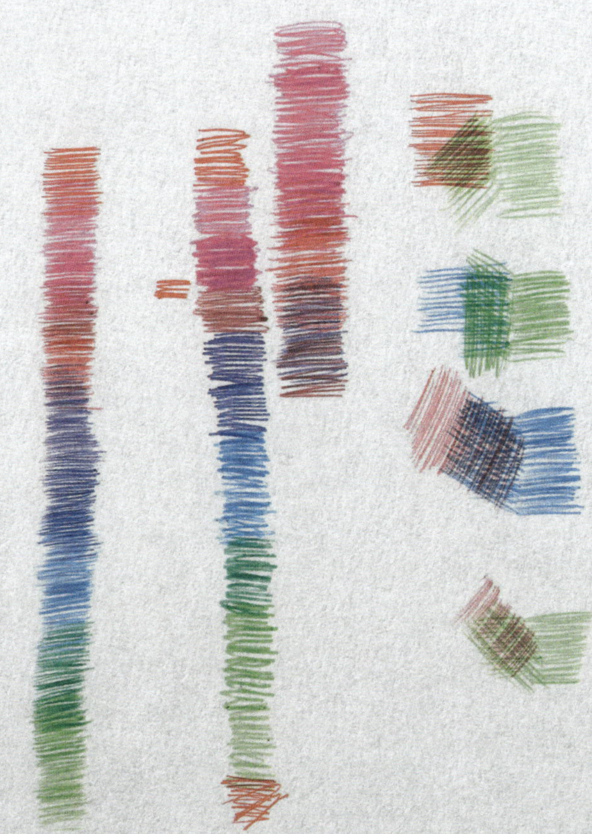

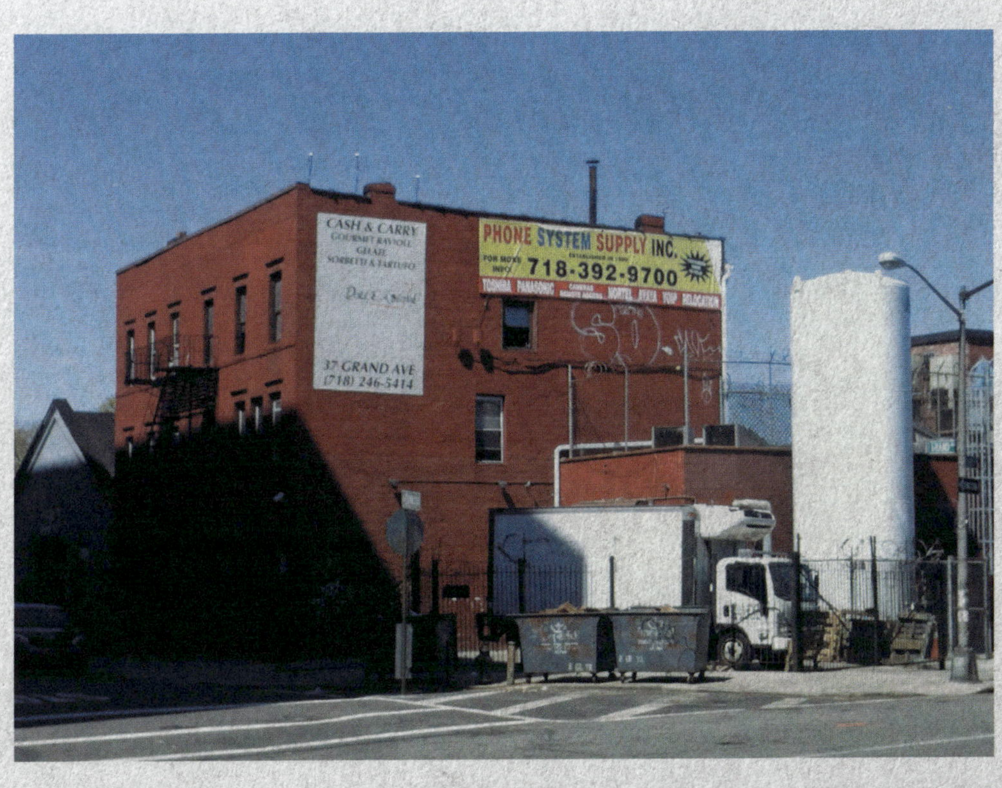
CASH & CARRY
37 GRAND AVE
(718) 246-5414
PHONE SYSTEM SUPPLY INC.
FOR MORE INFO
718-392-9700

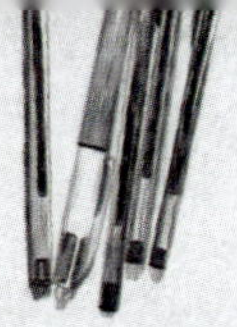

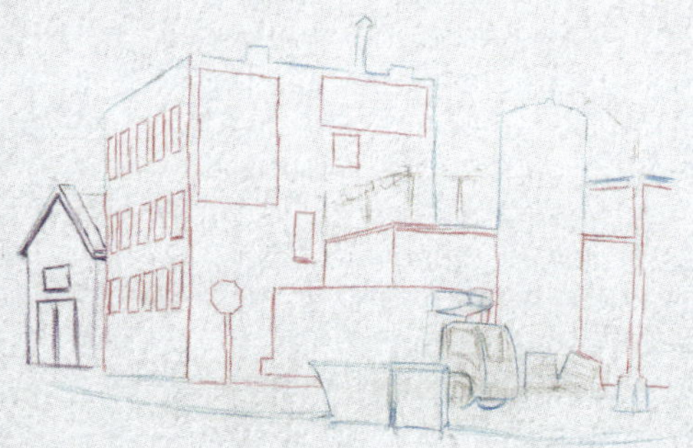

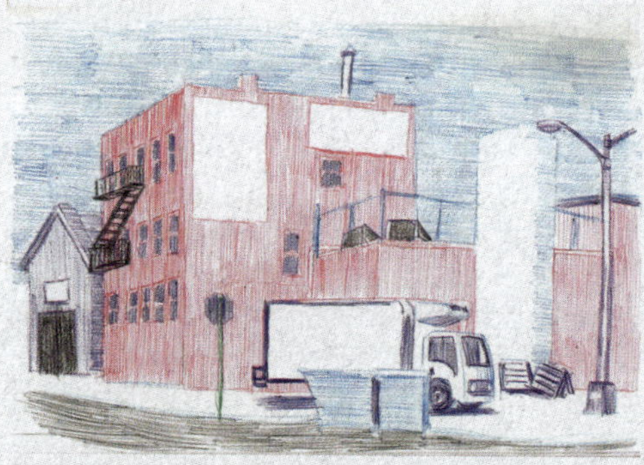

The way to achieve more complex colors is to layer them through crosshatching. The ink in ballpoint pens is fairly viscous, making it not very transparent, so layering in with dense marks won't blend new colors so much as quickly darken the drawing (there is not really any lightener in the form of ballpoint ink, except maybe in gel pens, so even though the colors are quite opaque, they darken as they layer). Crosshatching with light strokes creates a light, thin, and slightly transparent mark. Hatching a second color on top of the fist—say, blue over yellow—creates the sense of green in the overlapping and blending of ink, as with layering watercolor, but the sense of green is also created because in between the overlapping strokes is still visible pure versions of the yellow and blue. Up close, the colors are distinctly separate, but at a distance, the brightness of each color gives the impression of blending; like CMYK dots in a zoomed-in comic page, they separate into distinct colors, but at a distance, they blend together into a more complex and subtle palette. So when layering colors in ballpoint, it is important not to make heavy marks, but light, thin strokes.

When starting a color drawing, it may help to begin with a pencil sketch. The reason for a pencil sketch, as opposed to a preliminary drawing in ballpoint, is that every color is very visible at the end, so each object should be outlined with the specific color it will be drawn with, and it can be difficult to switch between several colors while trying to focus on building a composition.

Once the initial color lines are laid down, the first layer of color can be blocked in. These colors should tend toward the brighter and warmer side of the final color. In this case, the red building is the warmest color in the image. The color is not the red of the pen, but a deeper, cooler red, verging on purple in spots. The wall is in two main shades, a bright red on the left face of the building and a darker,

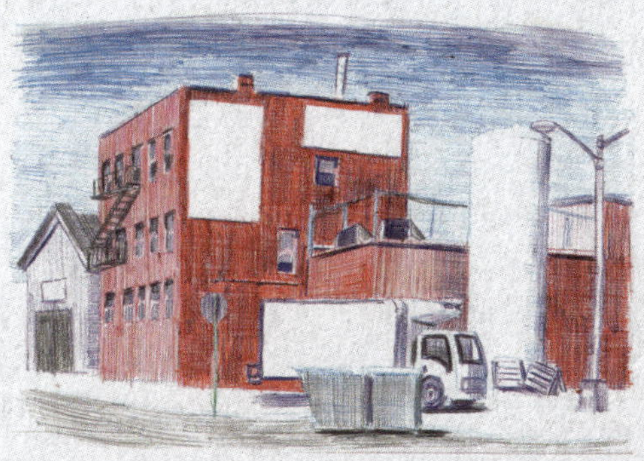

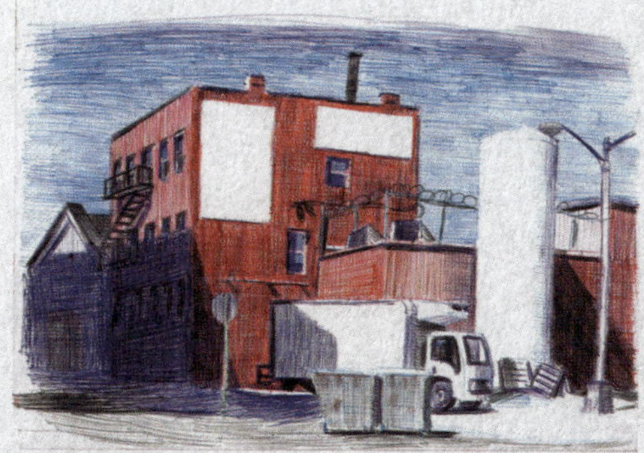

cooler color on the right. The color on the left more closely resembles the red from the pen, so the first layer of color can be applied more boldly here. On the right, the same red will have to be layered with purple to cool it down and resemble the color from the image, so the red should be applied more lightly. There is less red on this side than on the opposite wall, so more of the white paper needs to be exposed to display the purple that will be added in the second layer. The sky gradates from a dark blue to a light. It's not just a tonal shift, but also a color shift, from a purple blue to a slightly lighter more green blue. The colors don't need to be that specific, as the shift from a purple to a blue can be enough. The lighter of the two should be applied first.

The second layer of color will be darker and cooler. (It's easier to cool down warm colors than to warm up cool colors.) The pressure of the marks should be enough on this layer to make the form as dark as it needs to be. If the second pass of color does not make the surface dark enough, it's fine to work back and forth between the first color and the second one, building up the drawing until the balance of color and value is correct. (The red in the right wall had to be worked back and forth between purple and red a number of times to get the rich tone, and the same with the two blues used in the sky, whereas the left red wall was finished with only two passes, as were the Dumpsters in the foreground.)

The last step is to add the darkest, coolest colors. This layer is built up slowly so as not to overwork the shadows and turn them into black abstract shapes. Seeing the detail underneath (as in the windows on the left wall) creates a better sense of space, and it places the shadow on a three-dimensional surface.

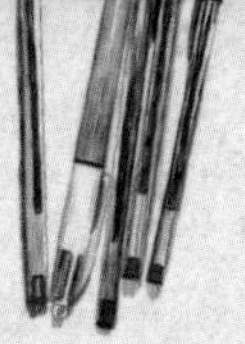

EXERCISE 9:

GRADIENTS WITH MARKS

THE CONSTRAINED NATURE OF THE BALLPOINT PROHIBITS CERTAIN FLEXIBILITIES THAT ARE INHERENT IN MEDIA DESIGNED SPECIFICALLY AS DRAWING TOOLS. THE ARTISTIC NATURE OF THE BALLPOINT PEN IS SECONDARY TO ITS PRIMARY FUNCTION AS A TECHNICAL TOOL. THIS LIMITATION PREVENTS THINGS LIKE LINE FLEXIBILITY; HOWEVER, THIS IS OVERCOME BY BUILDING UP FIELDS OF MARKS THAT CAN CREATE A SOFT-EDGED FEEL. ACHIEVING THIS SOFTNESS IS IMPORTANT IN CREATING GRADATIONS.

A field of marks created by ballpoint can, from a distance, give the impression of blending and a cloudy, atmospheric feeling; however, on close inspection, the soft gradating effect is achieved with a careful, graphic precision. A soft edge is usually achieved by gradually diminishing the pattern of marks.

This exercise looks at ways of achieving this diminishing effect with different marks. The process is similar to creating a field of marks. Start with drawing the extent of the field—or in this case, the gradation—and broadly spread out the marks for the gradation, leaving plenty of room to add more of the same mark in between the initial marks.

In the first example, start with a series of parallel lines, vertical or horizontal. Leave wide spaces in between them (this can actually be done numerically). Start with six parallel lines. Between the first two lines, fill in six lines. Between the next two lines, fill in half as much, or three lines. Between the next two, fill in one. This model acts as a close-up of how to think about diminishing lines at an even pace. On a larger scale, this idea can be used to create a smoother, more gradual gradation.

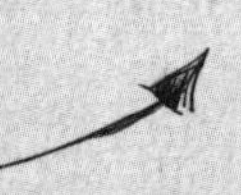

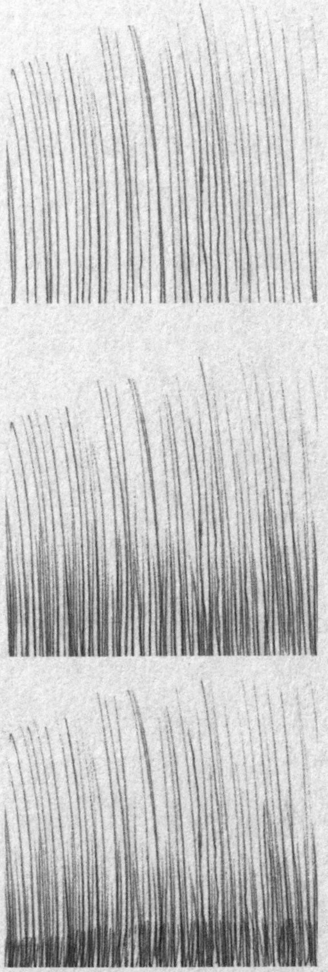

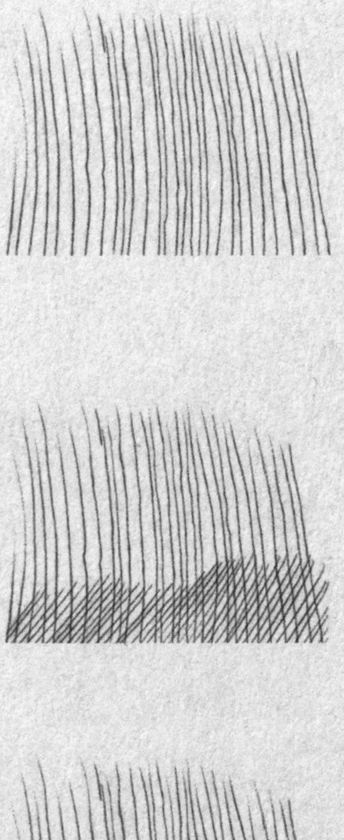

Another example of this can be done with a series of vertical lines. This time, make the lines more tightly arranged, but still leave room for more lines in between. Begin to add a new line in between every existing line, but only make the line half as long as the first set, so there will be an initial set of lines, longer than the rest, and a second row in between the first, but half as long. Continue adding lines in between each of the pervious lines, only half as long as the pervious set.

A third way to think about this is to begin the same as the last example, with a series of vertical lines, and then add a second series of lines half as long as the first, only this time hatch them over the first series at a 45-degree angle. Add another series half the length of the second series, hatching in at a 45-degree angle but moving in the opposite direction.

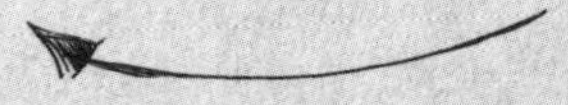

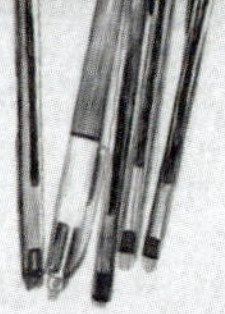

EXERCISE 10:

LINE SHAPE AND PATTERN

THE OBJECT OF THIS EXERCISE IS TO DEAL WITH A DRAWING IN PURELY GRAPHIC INFORMATION USING ONLY FLAT LINE, PATTERN, AND SHAPE (AS OPPOSED TO USING LIGHT OR VALUE TO DEFINE FORM, AND STIPPLING OR HATCHING TO DESCRIBE GRADATION AND VALUE).

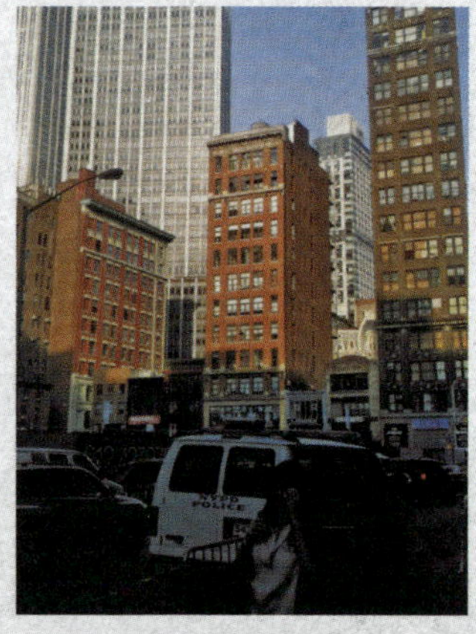

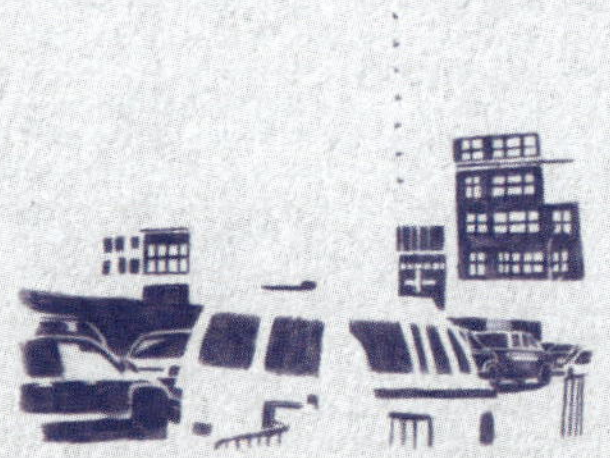

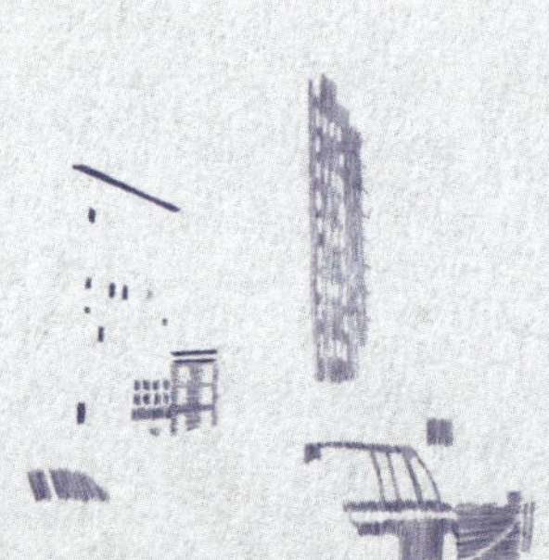

The subject must first be broken down graphically, which can be done by starting with a pencil drawing, though this is not necessary. In this drawing, any middle tone—that is, anything not a solid black shape or an outline—will be described by a graphic pattern (in the case of this image, parallel lines) that is flat and does not convey space.

First, identify how each shape will be treated: which ones will be outlines, solid shapes, or patterns. Next, draw the outline. All of the lines must be treated with an even weight. An even weight will abstract the line, making everything flat, understating the illusion of space, and bringing forward each element as an abstraction, calling attention to the abstraction instead of the illusion. In this particular example, the windows become as much an abstract pattern as the parallel lines used to describe the mid-tones.

Next, choose one of the other elements (solid shape or pattern) and fill it in everywhere it appears in the image. For instance, it may be best to first describe all of the solid shapes. Block in all of these to understand where the positive and negative areas will be. (This is easiest if you start with a pencil sketch of the composition.)

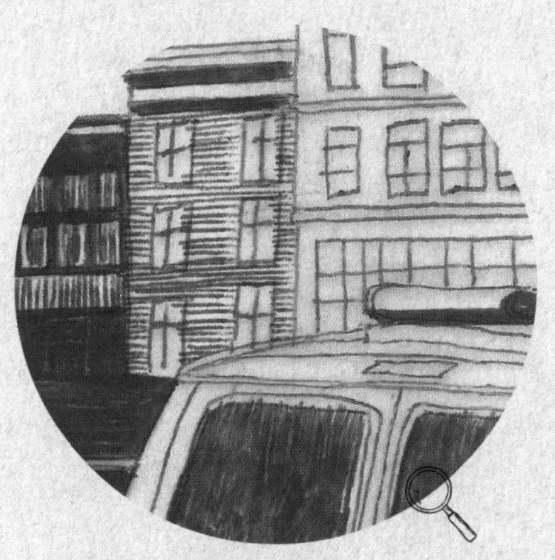

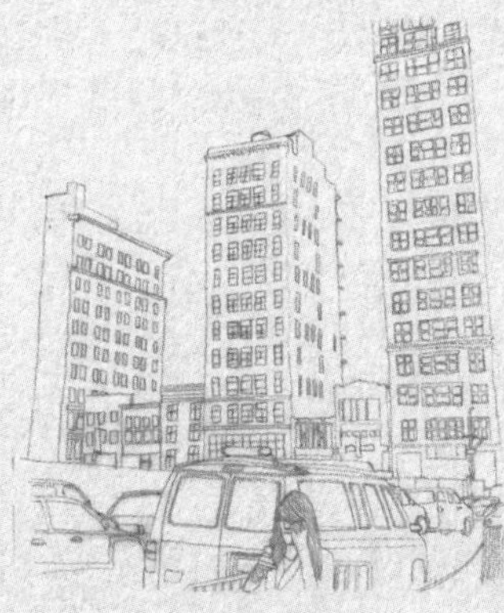

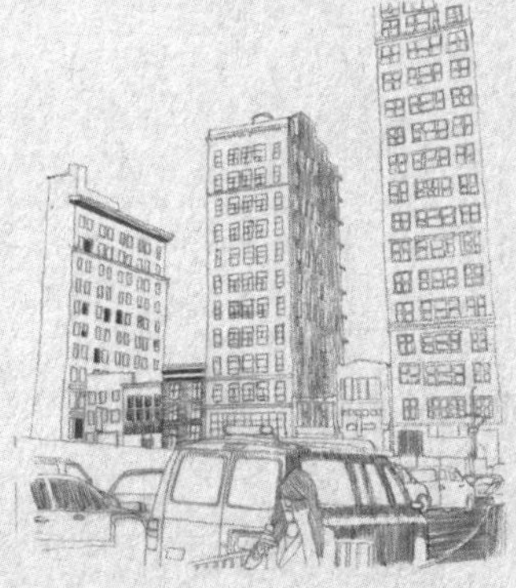

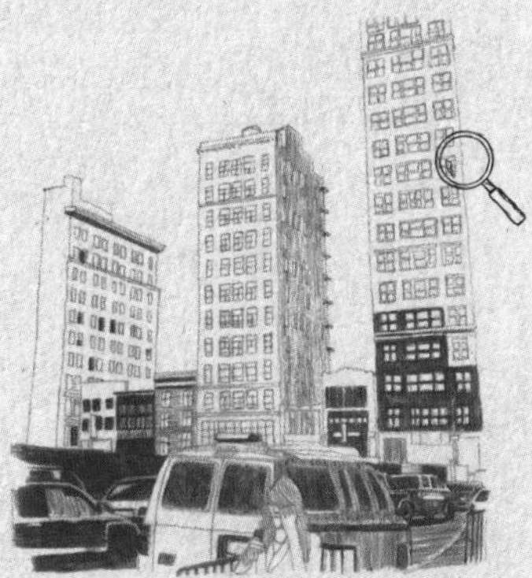

The parallel lines used to describe mid-tones could easily be replaced with another pattern. Here, parallel lines were chosen because they complement the vertical rise of the buildings. The pattern is laid out in a way to avoid gradation and the illusion of space, so each line is more or less evenly spaced to create a flat effect.

To create a sense of variety in the pattern, the areas of lines are varied from vertical to horizontal. A surface like the street stretches forward, so the lines are drawn in a horizontal pattern, to keep the van that is positioned next to the street from blending in with the street. The pattern of lines on the van is drawn vertically. The two surfaces are the same value, but distinctly separate objects.

The last step is to block in all of the darkest tones with solid, evenly rendered shapes, and all of these shapes must be completely filled in.

EXERCISE 11:

GRAPHIC COLOR

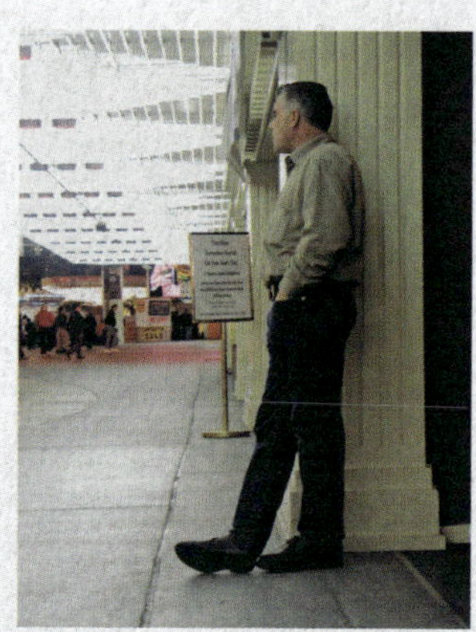

THE VARIATIONS IN BALLPOINT COLOR ARE NOT AS EXTENSIVE AS A MEDIUM LIKE COLORED PENCIL, SO THE COLORS TEND TO BE PRIMARY, SECONDARY, AND BOLD. EACH COLOR REPRESENTED IS IN A PURE FORM, UNLAYERED, AND THEREFORE UNBLENDED AND UNMUTED.

1

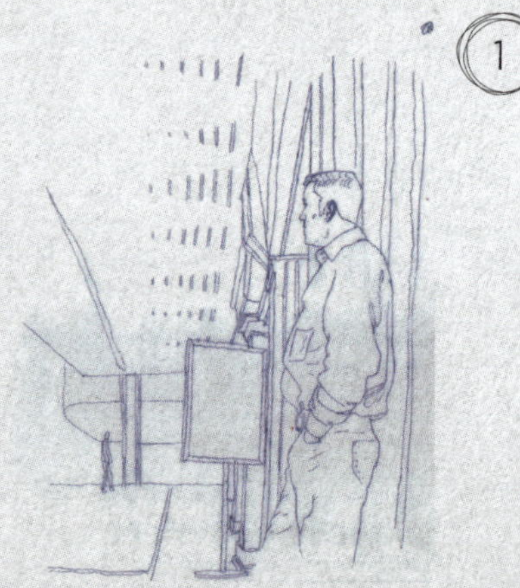

2

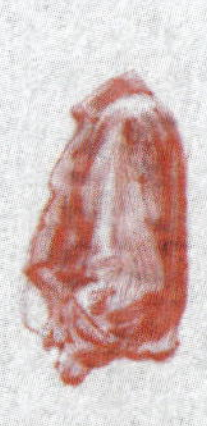

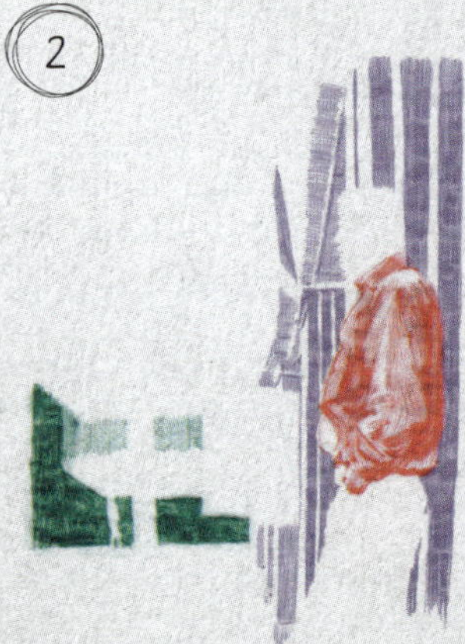

It's good to start with a pencil drawing to be certain of the composition, so you don't have to focus on the whole when dealing with the parts, though it is not necessary. A simple outline drawing is fine. The drawing should break down the composition into specific shapes—in this instance, the shirt, pants, face, floor, wall, and so on. The detail of each shape should be rendered in one color only, no blending of other colors to enhance shadows. Even though the color of each object is distinct, the value of the entire piece needs to make sense together. In this example, the red shirt still needs to be darker than the purple wall. These value relationships are important for maintaining the compositional structure of the image.

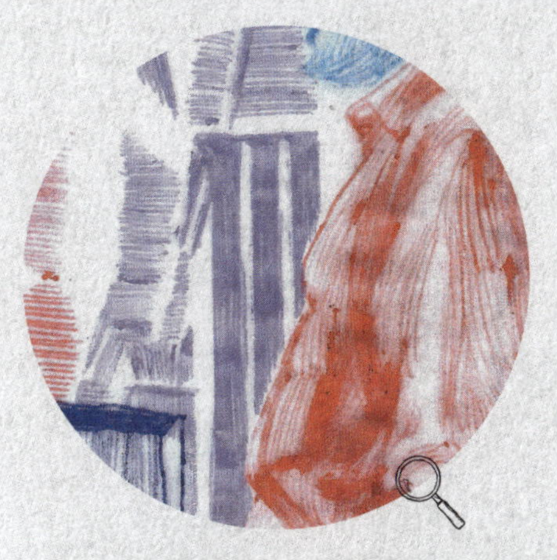

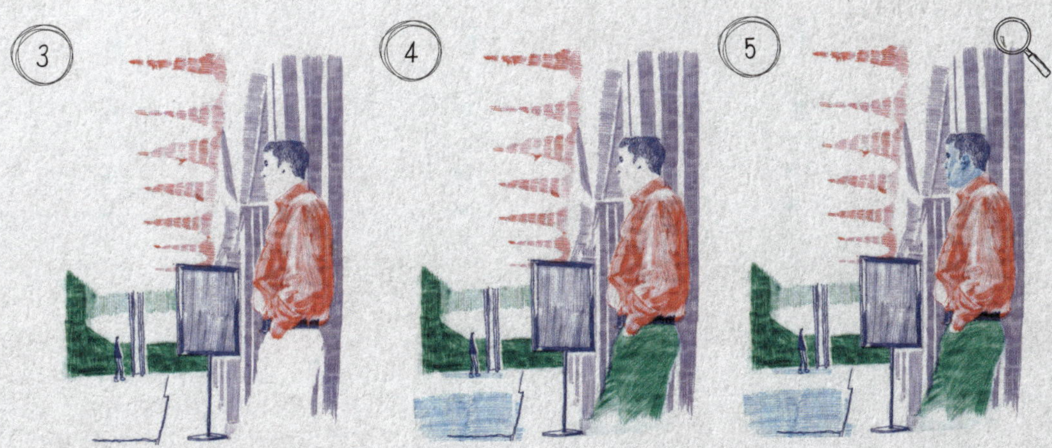

While breaking the image down into these basic elements, it is also interesting to consider the negative space by elements left out; for instance, consider leaving out the shirt, or the hair, or any combination of elements to see how much the image can be reduced and still be readable. While creating this drawing, consider what the basic elements the image needs are and what can be left out.

EXERCISE 12:

REPETITIVE MARKS

A MARK CAN BE USED TO CREATE AN ENTIRE FIELD OF SHADING OR BE REPEATED TO FILL A SPACE. THE OBJECT OF THIS EXERCISE IS TO EXPLORE VARIOUS WAYS TO USE MARKS TO CREATE PATTERNS AND REPETITIVE DESIGNS.

The easiest way to start is to create a single mark and then repeat it over and over to create a pattern out of it. Start with something simple and a simple set of rules. Use a short vertical dash. Create a row of this one mark and make sure the mark is repeated evenly and the row is a straight line.

Now begin a new row on top of the last, the same length and the same size mark. Continue to expand on this until the pattern begins to fill up the page. Be careful to keep the marks even so the pattern will be an even tone.

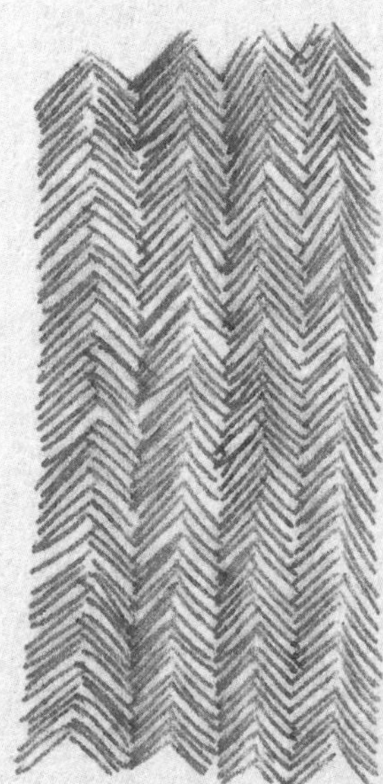

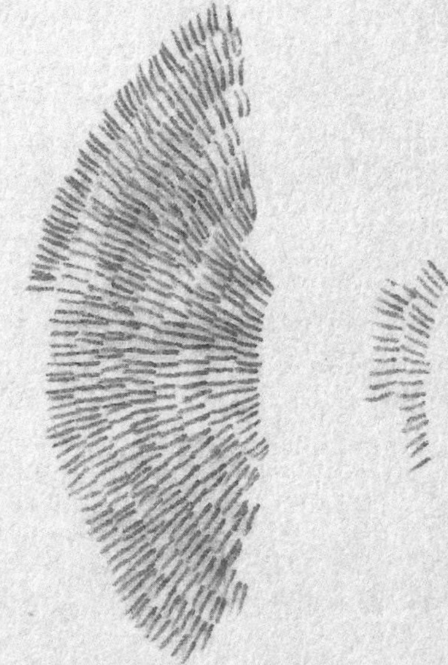

Next, take this mark and angle it at 45 degrees. Create a row of these marks. To make the pattern more interesting in the next row, create the mirror image of the mark, 45 degrees in the opposite direction, and begin to fill the page with this mark. The pattern, since it is basically the same mark as the first pattern, will from a distance be an even tone and the same tone as the first pattern, but on close examination, the alternation of marks is far more interesting because the zigzag pattern creates a sense of motion, rather than a stationary dash of the first pattern.

Now, explore more variations with this simple mark. Instead of rows on top of each other, draw a circle, and inside, around the perimeter, draw the dashes perpendicular to the line of the circle. This will begin to create an arch of sorts on the inside of the circle. Continue making concentric circles of dashes until the circle is full.

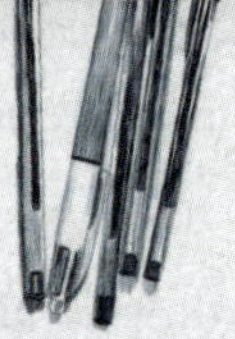

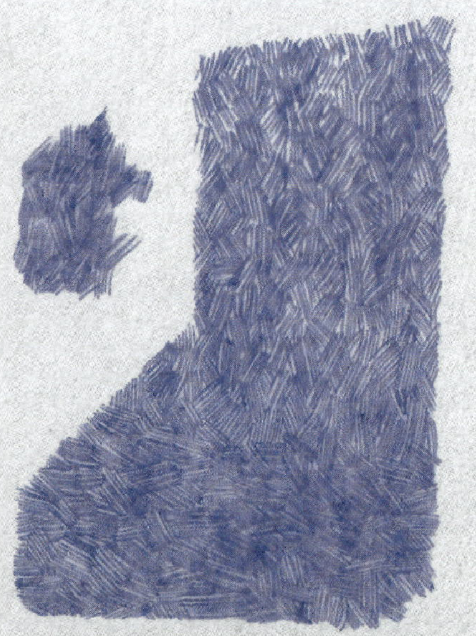

For something more complicated, create an asymmetrical shape and fill it with a dash pattern, but this time, use random angles, draw a series of four to six dashes in a row, and then in each subsequent series rotate the angle of the cluster so it is never the same as the previous one. This will create a random order of marks. Make sure you don't overlap the marks, or the pattern will become darker in areas and uneven. Each of these examples—the rows, the zigzag, the circle, and the random angles—will have a very different energy and expression; however, from a distance, they will all create the same even tone.

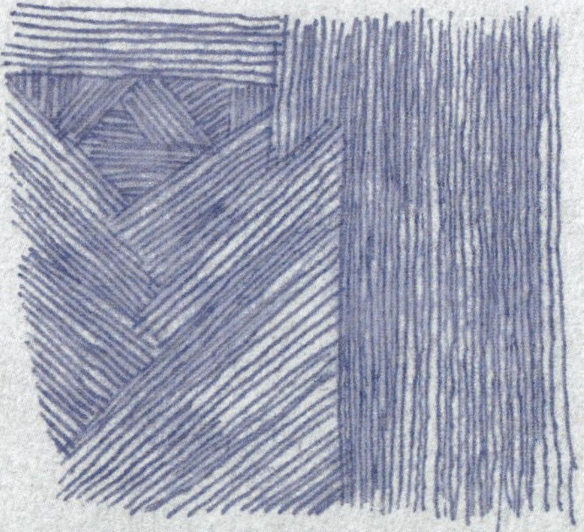

Try different ways of filling shapes using this idea of varying marks but making an even tone.

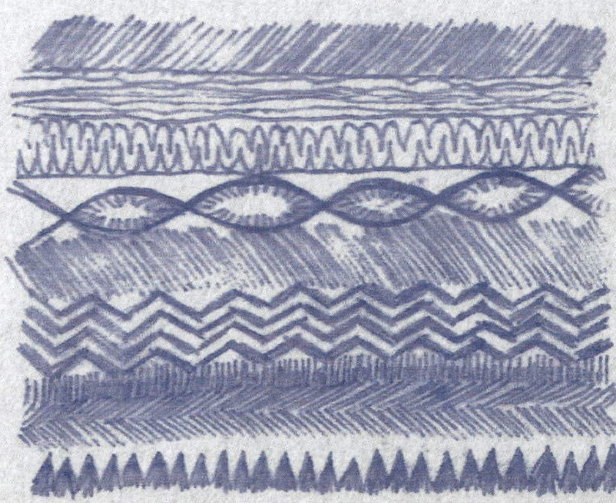

All of these examples are variations on a simple mark, which is rather conventional. Here's a game to play to discover new marks: create a single row of the same mark and then start a row of different marks on top of that. If the first row is 45 degrees, make the next row 90 degrees; if the previous rows had straight lines, then make the next row with curves. Try to keep the tone even and have each row contrast with the one below or above it. If any of the patterns leave white areas of negative space, modify the pattern to fill in the open space. This will encourage new ways of thinking about pattern making and encourage exploration and invention when trying to conceive new patterns.

GALLERY: ILLUSTRATION AND DESIGN

FEATURED ARTIST:

JIM RUGG

Jim references a wide range of subjects, which on the surface seem fairly unrelated, yet channeling them all through ballpoint pen into a notebook has a unifying effect, giving the sense of a single perspective. Connotations of childhood from the context of the notebook tie in nicely with the theme of the images: video games, superhero movies, and animals. These drawings are masterfully executed, but with the taste of a kid growing up in the late 1980s.

Below:
Abe Saplen, 2013
Pen and notebook
18 x 10½ inches (46 x 27 cm)

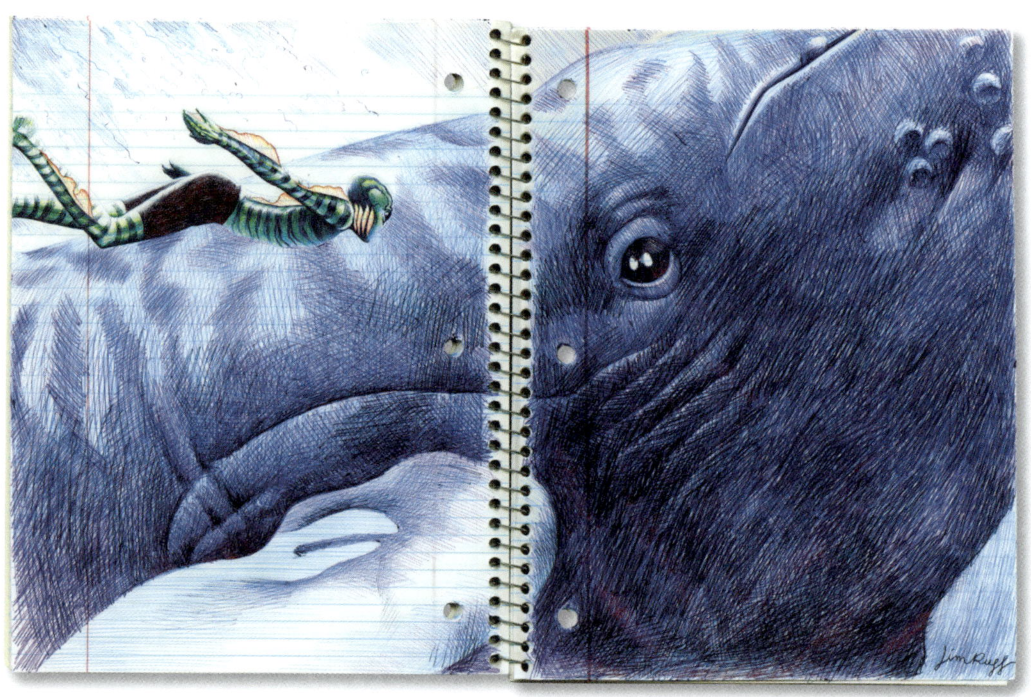

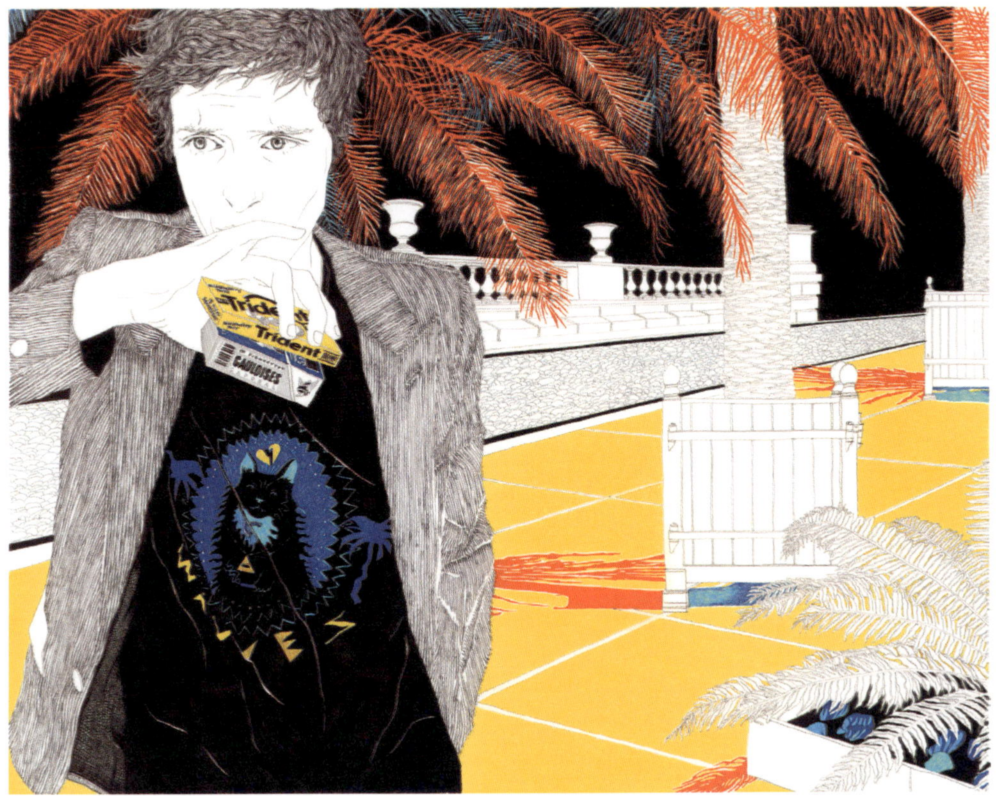

La Nouvelle Athnes, 2014
Pens on paper
47 x 31 inches
(120 x 80 cm)

FEATURED ARTIST:

CARINE BRANCOWITZ

Jim references a wide range of subjects, Carine Brancowitz creates drawings of fashionable young people in imaginary dreamscapes; her clean, stark style of drawing brings to life a sharp, ideal world. Figures and their environments are interpreted through clear delineations of line and pattern, hairstyles, clothing, and architectural and floral abstractions presented in bold simplicity. Her imagery combines a snapshot sense of intimacy in her subjects, with a fashion illustrator's sensibility toward the details and particulars of clothing and hairstyles. The figures, architecture, and plants have the simplicity, clarity, and idealism of an Athenian vase or of Greek and Roman sculpture.

FEATURED ARTIST:

CHAMO SAN

Chamo San is an illustrator from Barcelona; his work combines knowledge of classical figure drawing with a love of modern abstraction and graphic design. He uses ballpoint pen in a variety of techniques, including soft crosshatching, photo realistic tonal drawing, and flat graphic shapes.

In high school, he would draw all over his books and anything he had with a ballpoint pen, filling everything with drawings. He developed an interest in figure drawing and chose to study fine arts. Entering Barcelona University hoping for an education in technique, and the chance to explore new materials, he was disappointed with the experience. He later studied for a year in Paris, where he received better instruction in figure drawing. After finishing, he began to combine his knowledge of the figure with ballpoint techniques he remembered from high school, which led to a style steeped in detail and refinement.

Below:
Gatera II, 2014
Ballpoint pen on paper
12 x 12 inches
(30.5 x 30.5 cm)

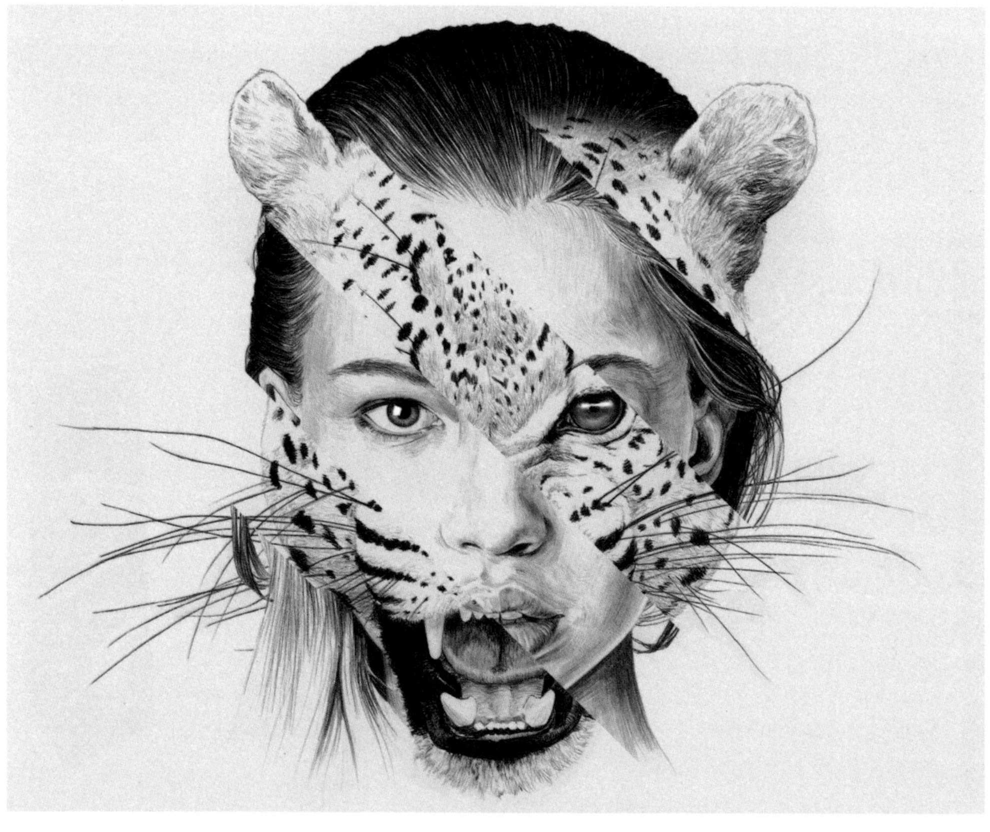

Right:
Untitled, 2000 Graphite, gesso, and ballpoint pen
7 x 10 inches (18 x 25.5 cm)

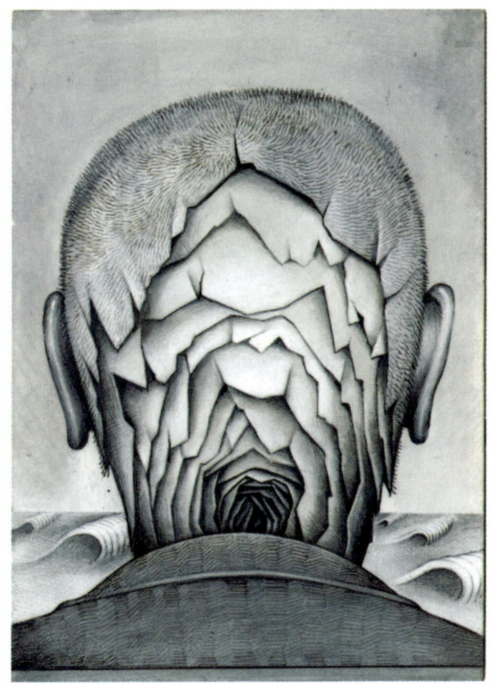

FEATURED ARTIST:

JOO CHUNG

Joo Chung worked as an illustrator for several decades and has taught drawing at the School of Visual Arts in New York for over twenty years. For his professional work, Joo typically relied on painting, but for his personal and sketchbook work, he uses primarily ballpoint pen. The pen is attractive for two reasons. The first is its convenience and availability. The other is that it does not need sharpening or refilling. After years of using a pen that needed to be dipped every so many minutes, Joo found the pause needed to dip his pen to be distracting, and he began to favor the consistency of ballpoint. Not having to pause during his drawing left him more in tune with his process, allowing him to become lost in his work.

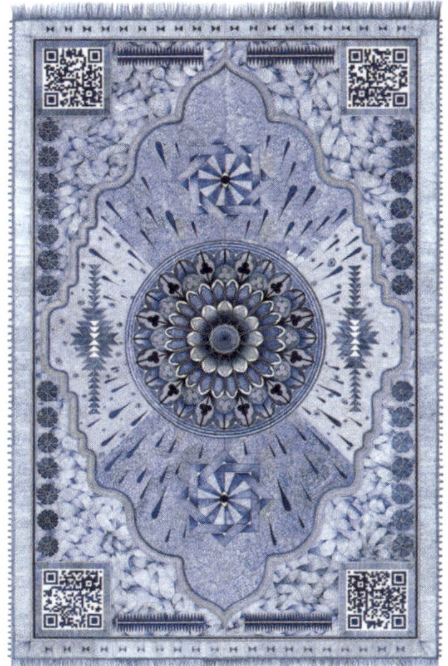

FEATURED ARTIST:

JONATHAN BRÉCHIGNAC

Jonathan Bréchignac's work combines abstractions and design elements from disparate sources: Quick Response (QR) codes, playing card suites, arabesques, and Southwestern American Indian art. Translating all of these symbols and information through ballpoint has a unifying effect, allowing otherwise disconnected symbols and design elements to feel natural, as though they belong together.

Left:
Carpet 6, 2013
Blue ballpoint, pencils, and UV ink on paper
45 x 29 inches
(115 x 73 cm)

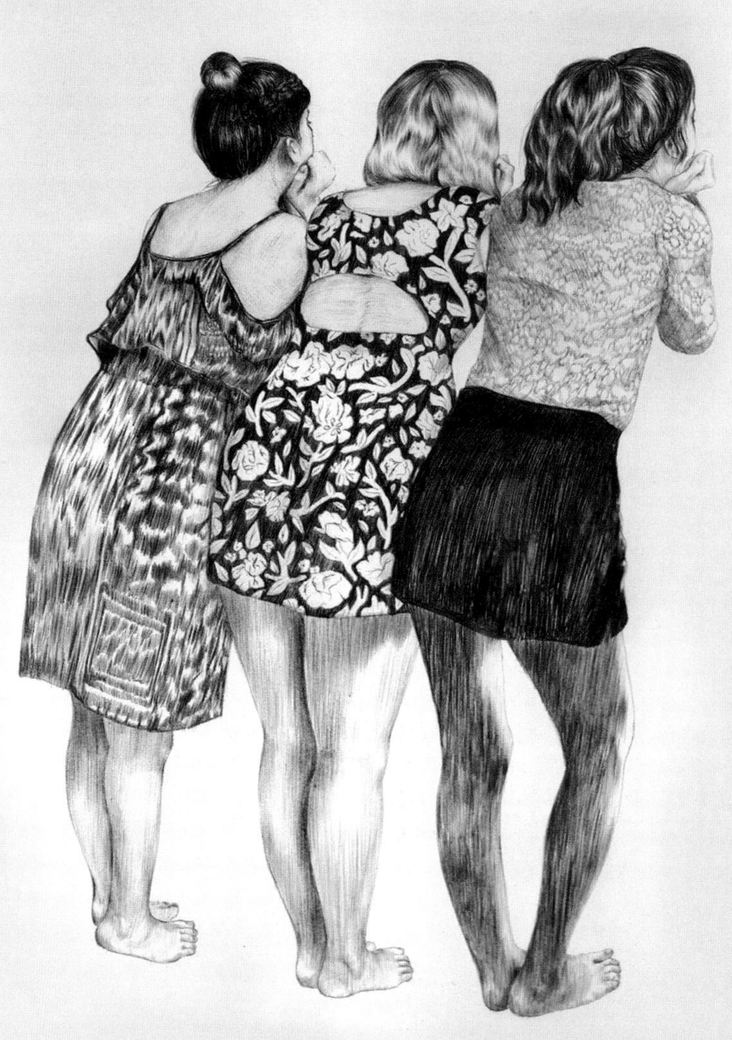

Melissa Ling
Untitled 9, 2012
Ballpoint pen
30 x 17 inches
(76 x 43 cm)

CHAPTER 4: SKETCHBOOK ART

In the past decade, there has been a surge of interest in sketchbooks and location drawings that revolve around the use of portable mediums. In this chapter, ballpoint is mixed with other media, such as watercolor for toning and white acrylic for highlights (similar to something a classical draftsperson would use). Some exercises layer images on top of each other and some explore the interplay between the observed and the imagined. What makes ballpoint unique to the sketchbook format is its durability, portability, and the fact that it is not messy and does not smudge easily.

EXERCISE 13:

CONTOUR DRAWING

THE OBJECT OF THIS EXERCISE IS TO CREATE AND LAYER CONTOUR DRAWINGS AND TO CREATE AN UNPREDICTABLE AND UNPLANNED COMPOSITION. LET YOURSELF BE LED BY THE LINE RATHER THAN COMPOSE AN IMAGE THAT FITS NICELY ONTO THE PAGE AND TRY NOT TO BE ATTACHED TO MAKING THE DRAWING THE PERFECT, MOST ACCURATE VERSION OF A SUBJECT. JUST FOLLOW THE LINE, AND LET IT DESCRIBE THE FORM NATURALLY AND ORGANICALLY. THIS EXERCISE IS A BIT LIKE WANDERING BLINDLY INTO A MAZE, AND IT HELPS ABANDON THE IDEA OF A "GOOD DRAWING" AND FOCUS ON THE ACT OF SEEING AND LOOKING RATHER THAN ON ACCURACY OR BEAUTY.

1

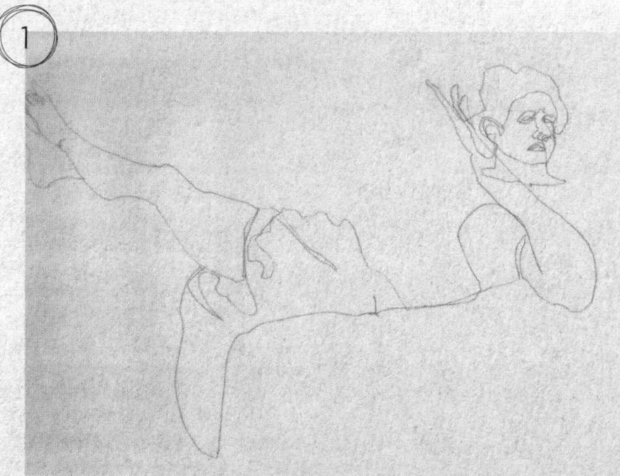

The basic rules are to use the line to follow the form of the subject. Make one line, with the pen not leaving the paper, until the form is complete. If the line reaches the end of a subject but the form is not complete, without retracing over old lines, find creative ways of connecting the line with the remaining portions of the subject without lifting the pen or creating a new line. This may mean drawing through the figure and creating lines that are not in the subject. There are no right ways of completing a drawing like this, and it may go against the artistic instinct that you will "ruin" a drawing this way, but it forces you to consider new ways of using line. It also creates a deliberate limitation, an obstacle in the creation of a drawing, so it forces you to break out of traditional thinking about drawing, to work with the options at hand. Limitations such as these help enhance an artist's understanding of what is possible with very few choices.

2

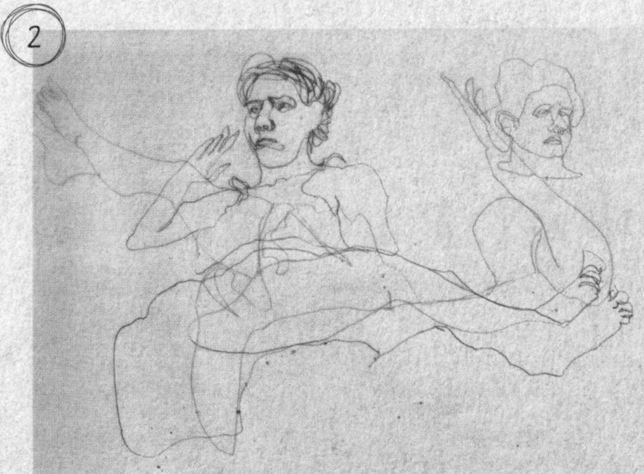

Once the initial form is captured, change position and look at the subject from a new point of view. Begin the second rendering directly on top of the first, following all of the same limitations. This will start to create a scribble effect, where the lines that may have clearly described the previous subject will be lost or abstracted by the layering.

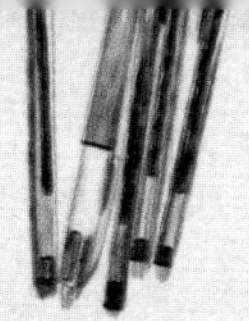

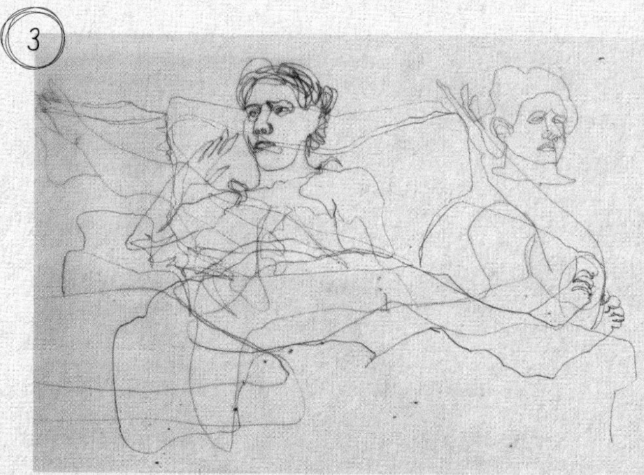

3

Continue to layer this way through several position changes. The composition will become dense and further abstracted. Some elements, such as the face in this example, will remain clear, while other portions will become obscured. Experiment with different colored pens as well.

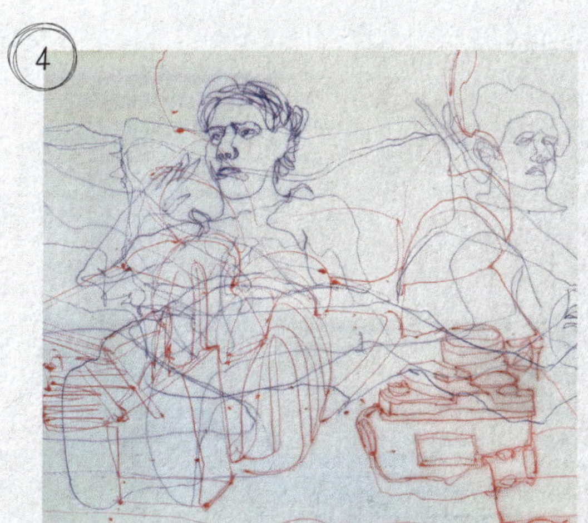

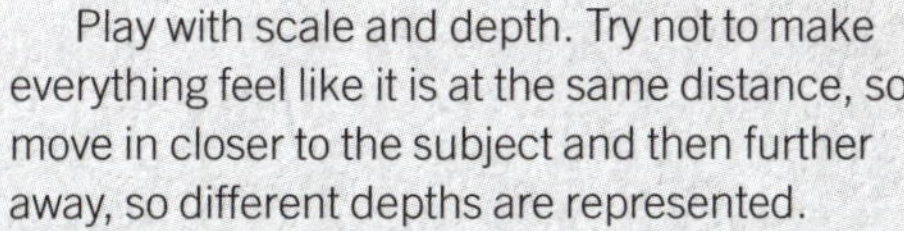

Play with scale and depth. Try not to make everything feel like it is at the same distance, so move in closer to the subject and then further away, so different depths are represented.

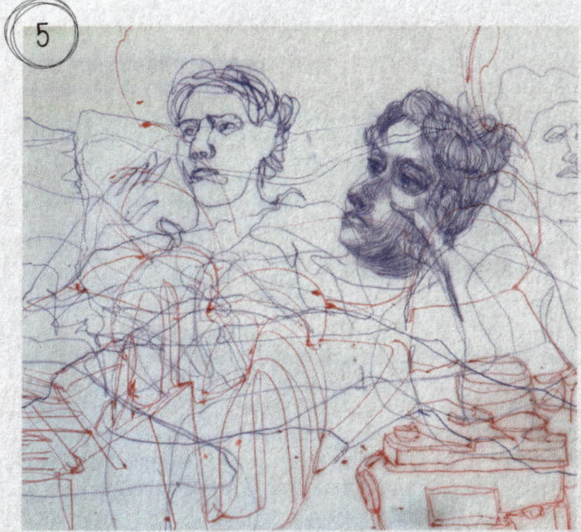

Once the composition is full, it may be helpful to spend time developing portions of the drawing further, now using more complicated shading. At the end, feel free to break the previous rules and layer a more complete and rendered drawing over the scribbled layers of contours. This will force you to work on top of other lines, and across the contours underneath, again presenting obstacles in composing a more perfect drawing.

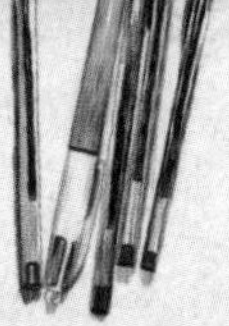

EXERCISE 14:

CREATING A LIGHT SOURCE

UNDERSTANDING HOW THE VOLUME OF AN OBJECT WORKS HELPS TO UNDERSTAND HOW TO CONTROL THE LIGHT THAT FALLS ON THE OBJECT.

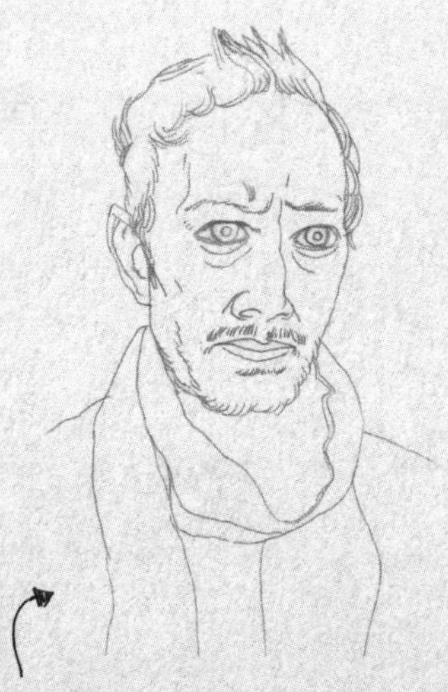

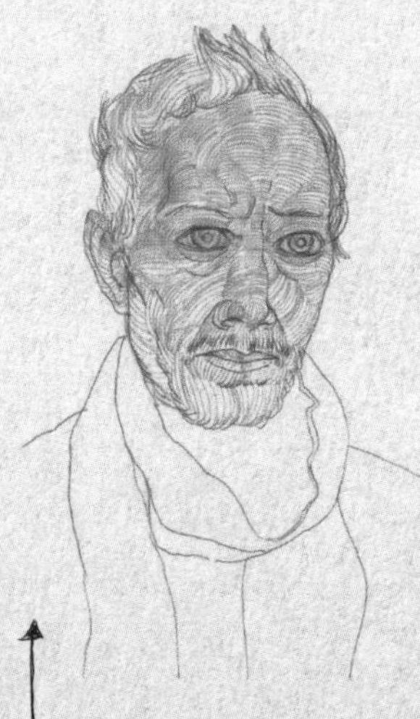

To begin this process, the drawing must be done only in line, with no tone. It may help to do a pencil drawing first. This drawing should be over-rendered to overstate the muscle and bone structure underneath the surface of the skin in the portrait. Understanding the placement of the muscles will help describe the shadows later on and help you understand how shadows fall across them under different light sources.

To understand how lines describe the shadow, cover the surface with even lines as if a shadow were covering the entire face. Use this as a study to guide how shadows will fall under different light sources. In a separate drawing, experiment with inventing a light source.

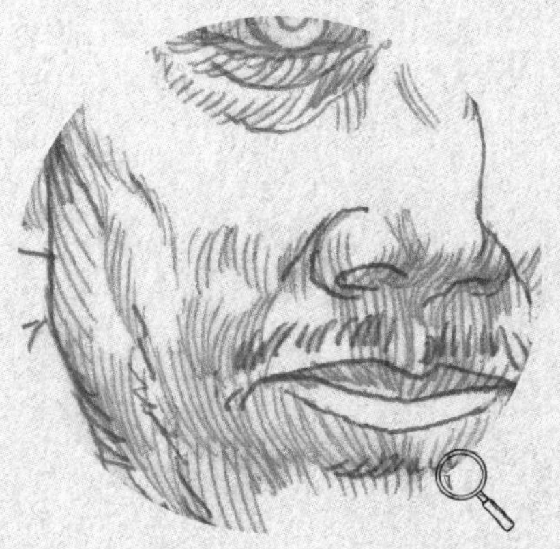

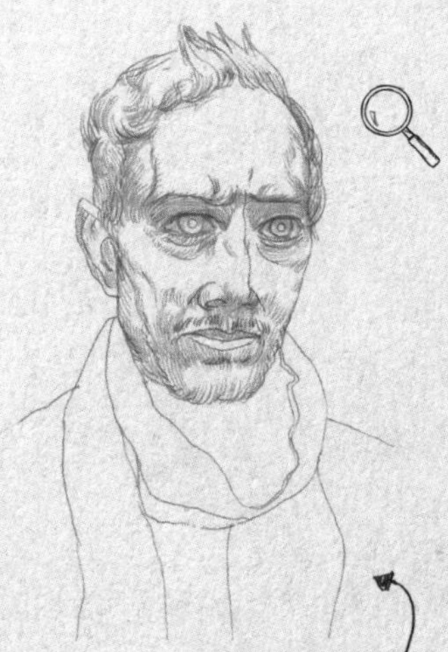

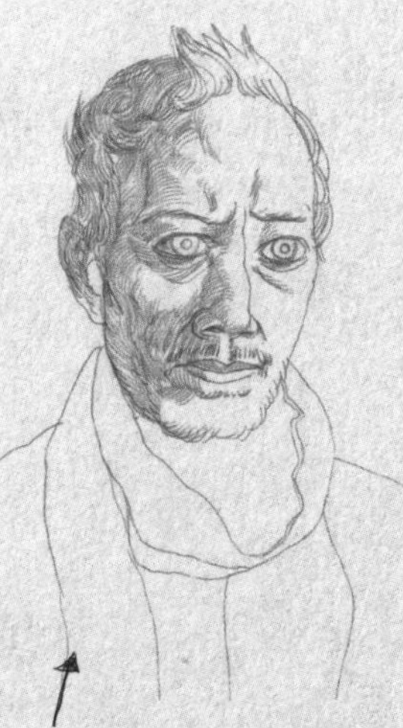

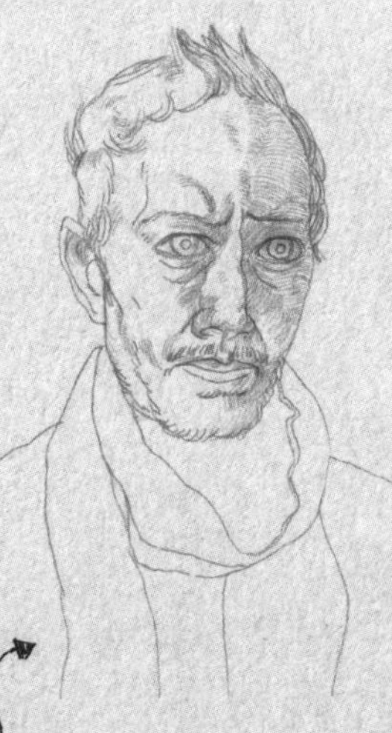

Begin with a light source from above. Cast shadows under the eyebrows, nose, and lips, following the guides in the previous study. Experiment in this same manner from different angles.

Next, show a light source from the right.

Finally, show the same image with a light source from the left.

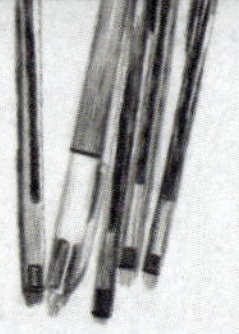

EXERCISE 15:

SHADING WITH WATERCOLOR

TRADITIONAL BALLPOINT PENS SUCH AS THE BIC BRAND USE OIL-BASED INK, A THICK WATERPROOF MEDIUM. THERE ARE ALSO ROLLERBALL PENS, WHICH ARE SIMILAR TO THE BALLPOINT IN THE TIP AND DISPENSATION METHOD, BUT THE INK IS EITHER A GEL OR WATER BASED. IT'S AN IMPORTANT DISTINCTION IN THE EVENT OF MIXING INK WITH A WATER-BASED MATERIAL LIKE WATERCOLOR. WATERCOLOR CAN BE USED WITH TRADITIONAL BALLPOINT, AS THE INK CAN BE PAINTED OVER AND WON'T BLEED, BUT IN ROLLERBALL PENS, SUCH AS THE UNI-BALL OR PILOT, THE WATER-SOLUBLE INK WILL RUN.

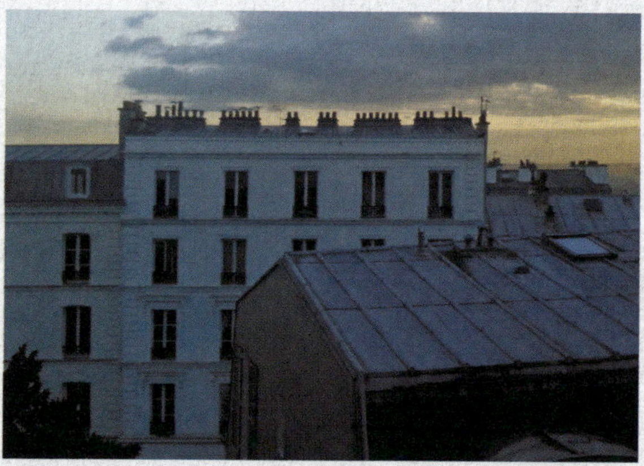

Although ballpoint ink is waterproof, it is good to check it with water first on a scrap sheet of paper. Even though it is oil-based ink, there is still a bit of bleeding that can occur when water is added. It is minor, but if a colored ink is being used, it may interact with the watercolor to create an unexpected tint, and it can also make the lines of the drawing swell mildly, creating a slightly heavier line than anticipated.

The goal of this exercise is to explore how to use watercolor and ballpoint together. Watercolor can act as a good toning and shading medium. When using watercolor to paint over ballpoint, it is important to start the drawing with the intention of adding watercolor later. This means knowing what the watercolor will be used for and to leave room open for it in the drawing. If watercolor will be used to create shadow, then the ballpoint drawing should be only in line. It is redundant to add shadow with two different mediums. If you indicate shadows in an image by, say, crosshatching, then it is perhaps repetitive to add tone in the same area with watercolor.

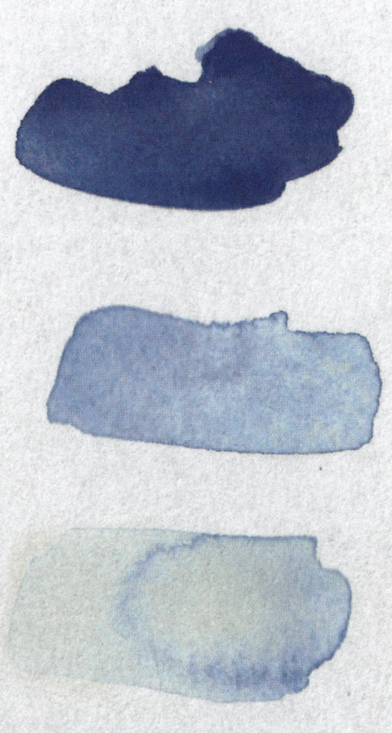

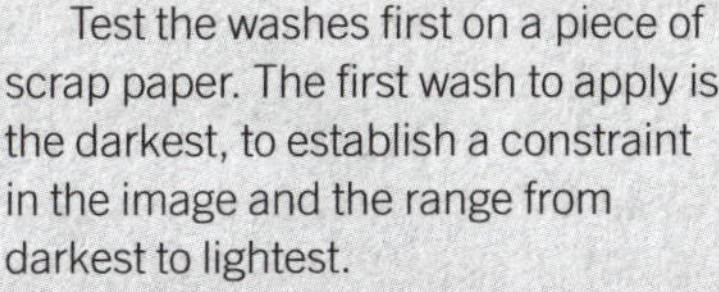

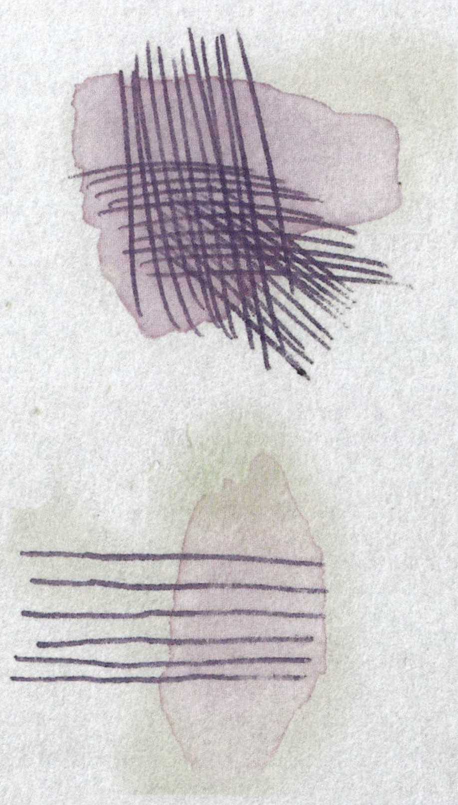

Test the washes first on a piece of scrap paper. The first wash to apply is the darkest, to establish a constraint in the image and the range from darkest to lightest.

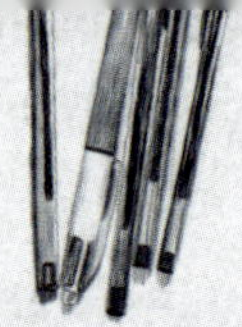

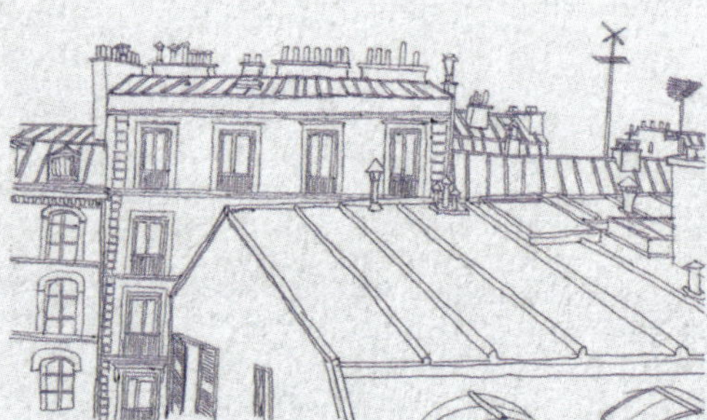

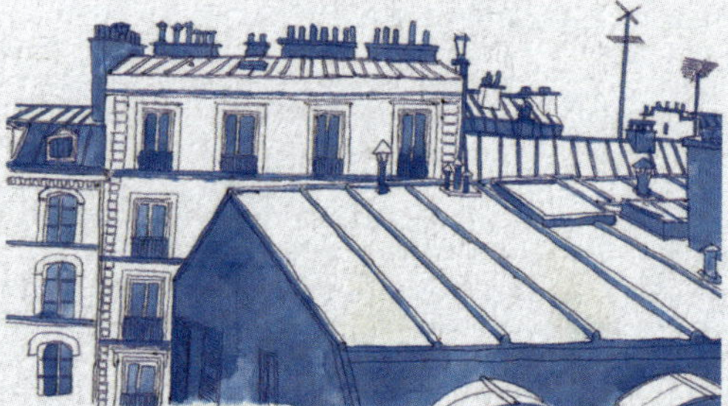

Create a drawing completely out of line, describing only shapes and contour, no shadow. To keep things clear and simple, the watercolor should be divided into three values: a dark value, a mid-tone, and a light, almost transparent shade. More than this runs the risk of making the image murky. The subject may have a wider range of tones, but this is an easy way of simplifying the information from the start.

To understand a clearer sense of the values in the subject of the drawing—to simplify the information as much as possible—it helps to squint at the subject so that all of the detail disappears, and all that is left are the more general pieces of information. This makes it easier to identify which forms will be described by the three tones (white is the fourth tone, in fact, so always leave the white of the paper for the whitest white).

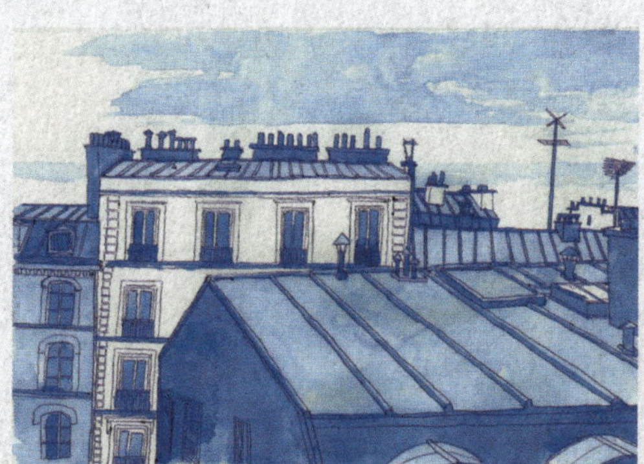

To identify the next two tones in the subject, think of the lighter of the two, the next lightest value other than white. Consider all of the lightest parts of the image that are not white, and paint these with the lighter of the two remaining values. The remaining value will be the mid-tone.

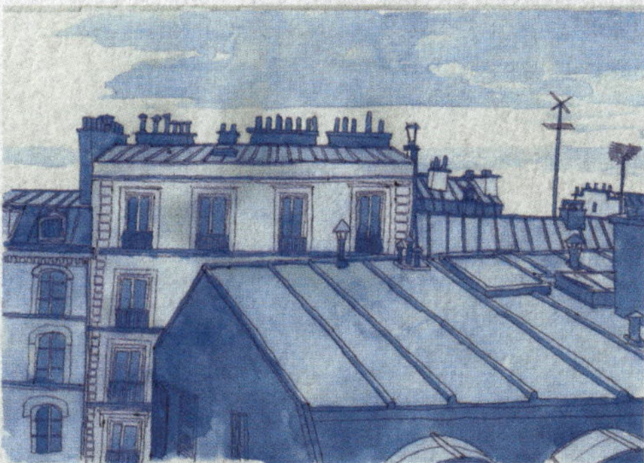

Once the image is broken down into these three values (four with white) this can be the end of the image, or it can be the ground upon which more refined detail is built.

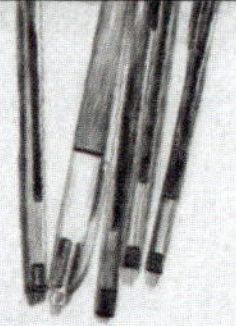

EXERCISE 16:

LAYERING BALLPOINT AND ACRYLIC

ACRYLIC IS A GOOD MEDIUM TO USE FOR ADJUSTING BALLPOINT PEN. BECAUSE BALLPOINT HAS NO ERASER, CLEANING UP MISTAKES ARE OTHERWISE IMPOSSIBLE. THERE ARE TWO WAYS TO USE ACRYLIC ON BALLPOINT: OPAQUELY AND TRANSPARENTLY. OPAQUE IS GOOD FOR FIXING MISTAKES, BRINGING OUT THE WHITE OF THE PAGE, AND ADDING SHARP HIGHLIGHTS. TRANSPARENT IS FOR ADDING DEPTH, PUSHING LINES BACK IN SPACE, AND GENERALLY CREATING MORE DEPTH.

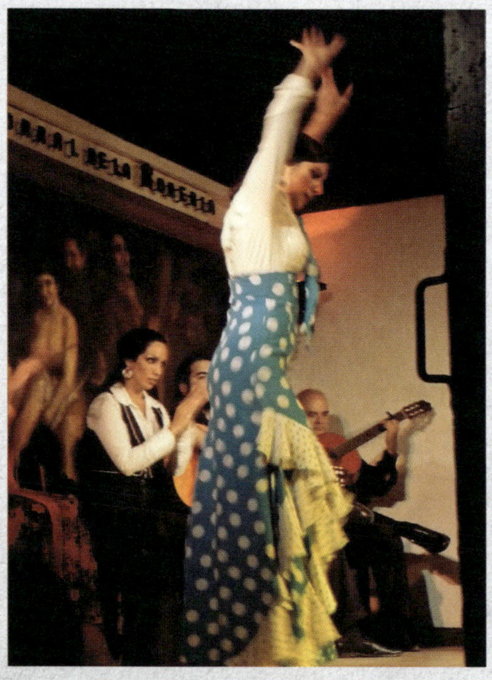

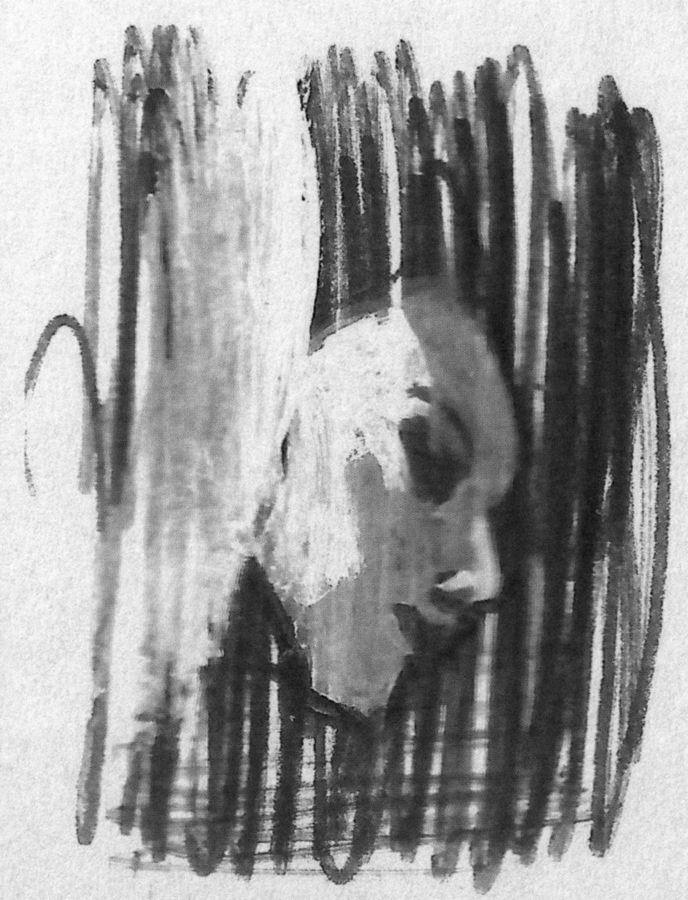

To test how this works, create a square filled in with ballpoint so it is dark. Look at a photo or draw from life and focus only on the highlights of the subject. Allow the dark of the ink to be the shadows and pull out the highlights with acrylic. Start with a wash to describe the forms and add the opaque for the true whites. This will give an idea of how the two materials relate to each other.

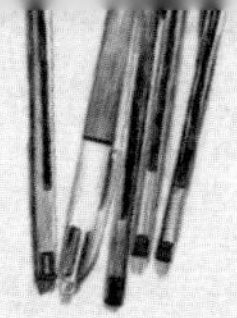

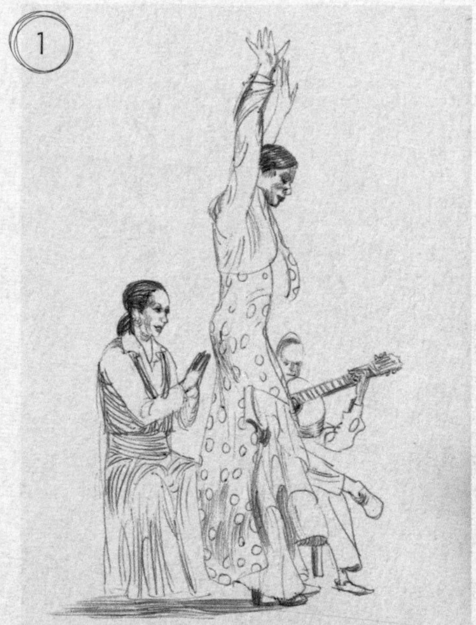

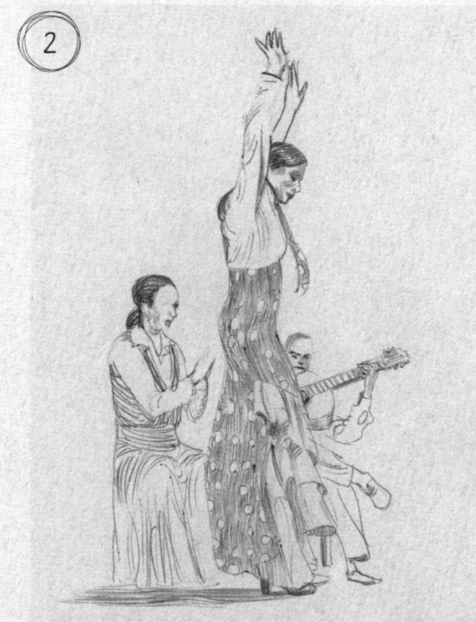

For a larger example, create a ballpoint drawing that is fully composed but not resolved. The drawing is one that will be refined, so draw it quickly and use a lot of energy; this is not a precious drawing, but a loose sketch that will be built up over time. There should be no pencil drawing, so draw straight to paper with pen and do not labor over mistakes.

The next step is to refine the areas where mistakes were made or where detail is to be focused. The end product will be a drawing that goes from tight to loose, with areas of spontaneity next to refined drawing. Hands and faces are perfect areas to focus on and refine. Cover up the areas that are incorrect or disproportional with acrylic. Ballpoint draws very nicely over acrylic, so the texture of the marks will be more or less the same as they appear on paper.

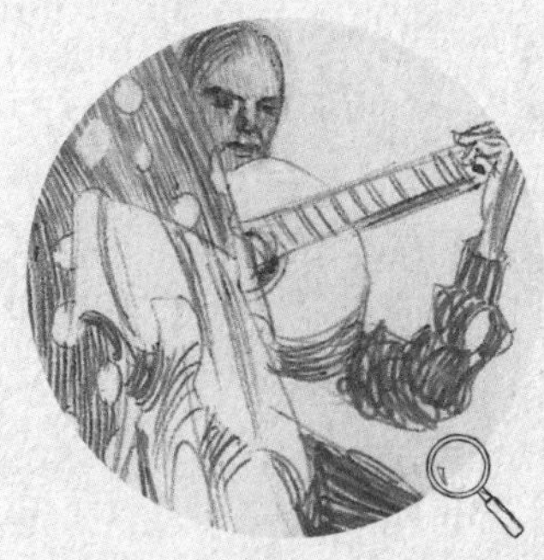

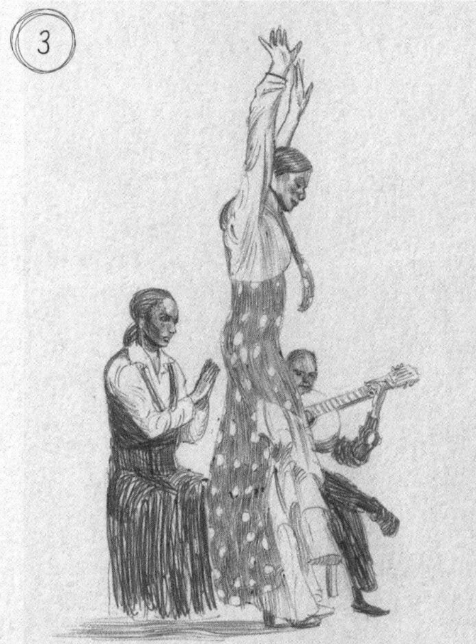

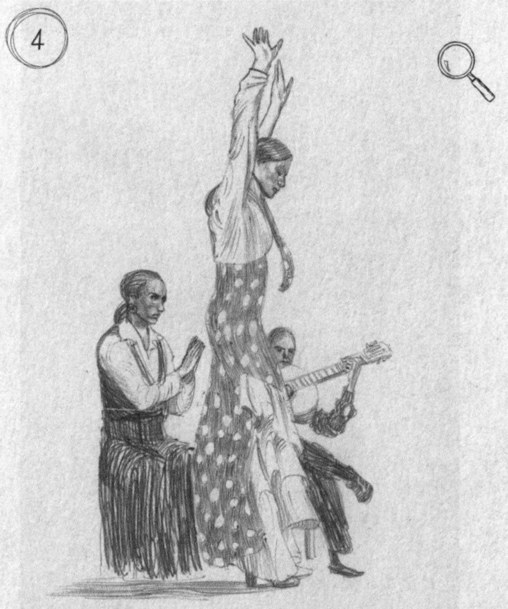

Once the acrylic dries, continue to rework in pen over the painted areas and build up the rest of the drawing along with these painted areas. Lightly washing a transparent layer over the ballpoint will soften it as well, and lend precise areas a more delicate feel giving the illusion of a more tonal drawing, almost like a painting. Building lines on top of that will create a deeper tonal range.

As the details of the lights are added by working back and forth over the painted areas, continue to develop the looser areas of the drawing with no paint. Focusing on only one area will give a false impression of how finished it is. If an area is not developed in relation to the rest of the values, having a very finished head does no good if the body is not resolved. If the detailed areas are finished first and then the rest of the drawing follows, once the whole is complete, the focused areas' relationship to the rest of the image will look awkward. The "finished" head will not fit properly and will need to be worked on more, and it then risks being overworked.

GALLERY: SKETCHBOOK ART

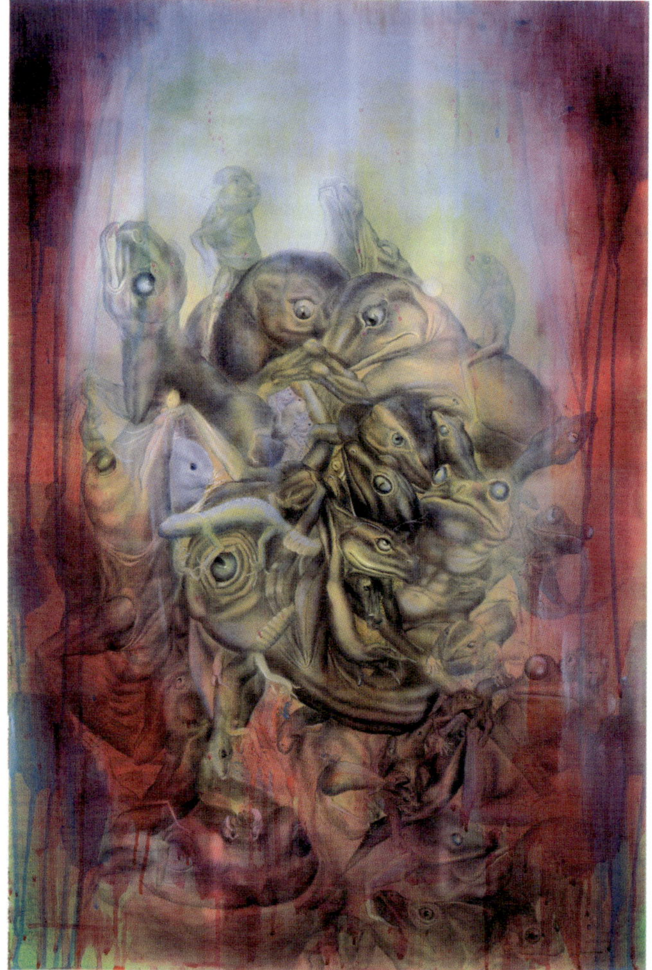

FEATURED ARTIST:

JEAN-PIERRE ARBOLEDA

Jean-Pierre is primarily an oil painter. He works in ballpoint for drawings and sketches. Working on paper toned with watercolor, he uses acrylic washes for depth and highlights.

Left:
Sapicidio II, 2008
Ballpoint pen with acrylic on paper
45 x 32 inches
(114 x 81 cm)

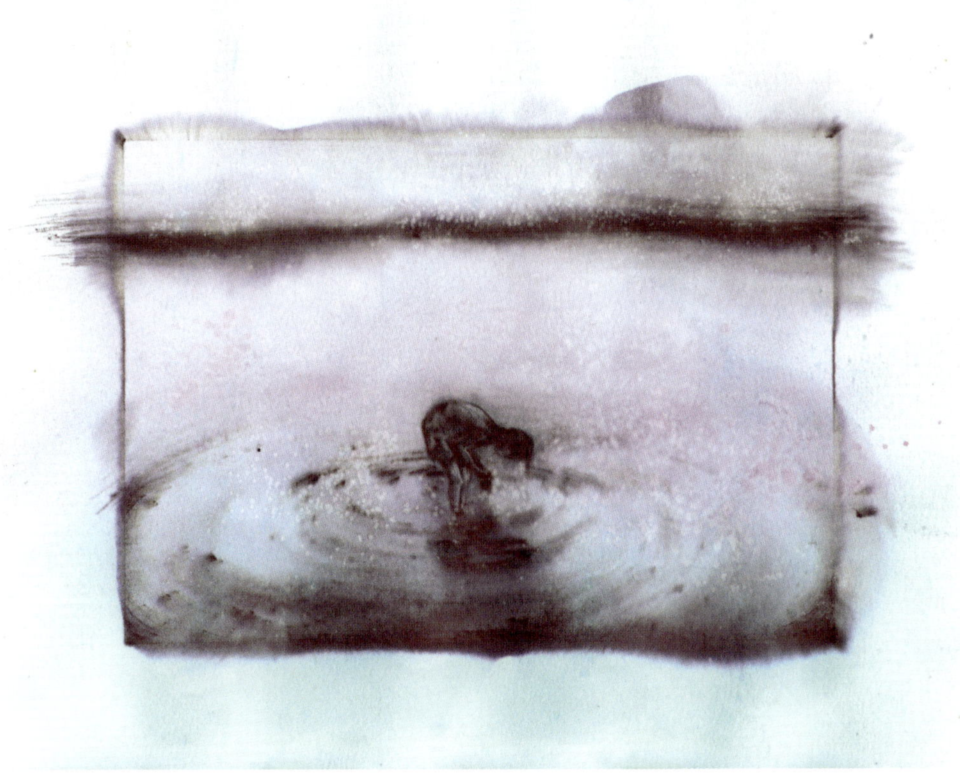

Above:
For K&J 2, 2011
Ballpoint pen, acrylic, and watercolor
6 x 8 inches
(15 x 20.5 cm)

FEATURED ARTIST:

MELISSA LING

Melissa Ling is a narrative artist working mostly in the field of illustration. Her work combines an assortment of mediums, including acrylic, oil, charcoal, graphite, and ink. Her illustrations appear in magazines, and she self-publishes handmade books of her work, exhibits her drawings in galleries, and keeps regular sketchbooks.

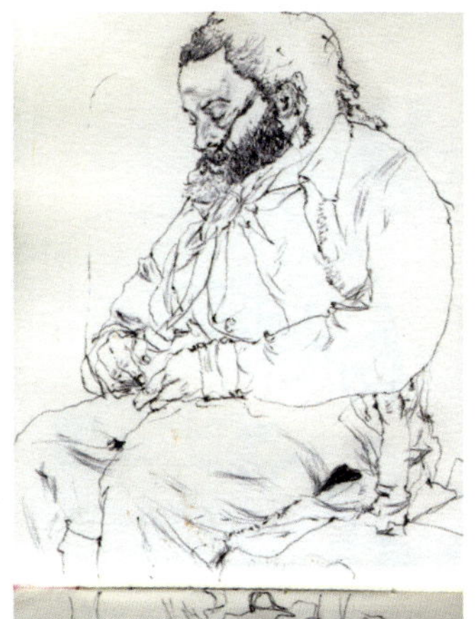

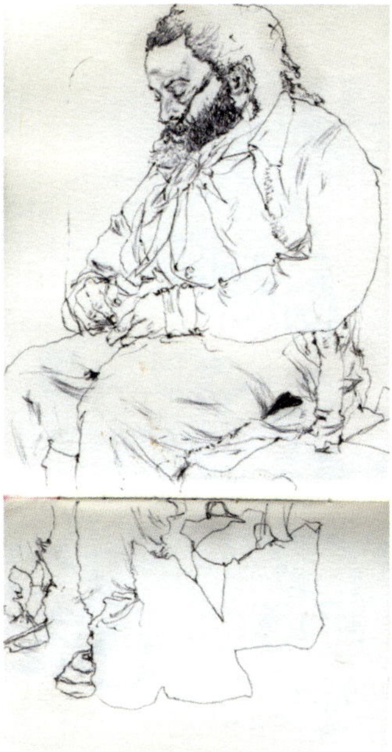

Left:
Sketchbook Portrait, Man Sitting, 2009
Ballpoint pen on paper
4½ x 11½ inches (11.4 x 29.2 cm)

FEATURED ARTIST:

MU PAN

Mu Pan is best known for his elaborate, large-scale acrylic and watercolor paintings that fuse Japanese, Chinese, and American histories and popular cultures into epic allegories with no distinction between history and imagination. Mu's oldest tool of choice, however, is the ballpoint pen.

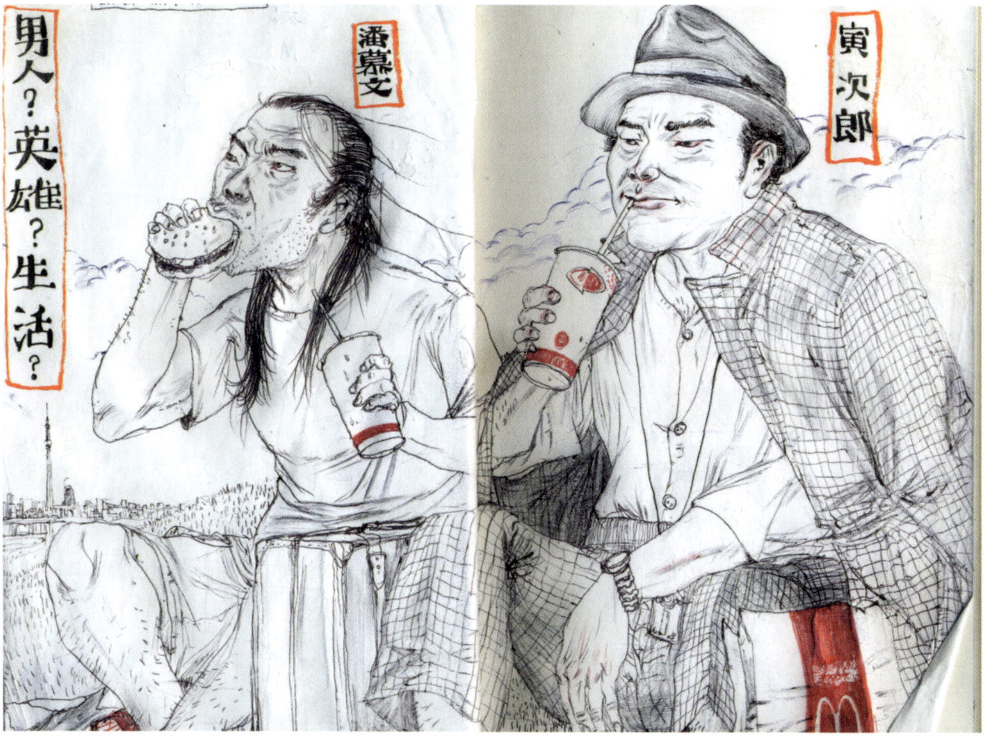

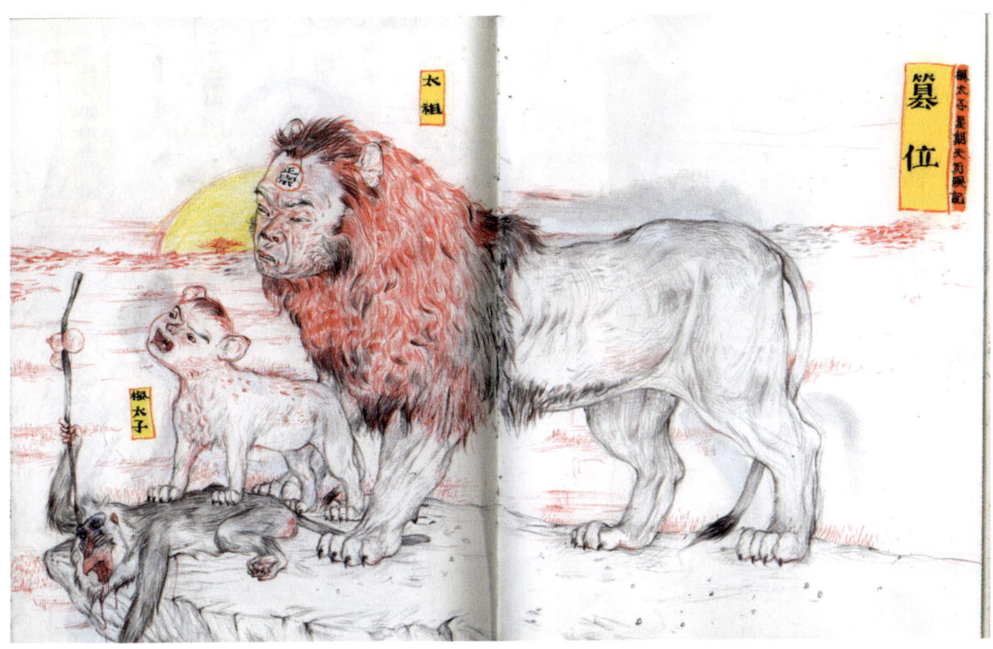

Opposite:
Lunch with Tora San, 2014
Ballpoint pen on paper
9 x 6 inches (23 x 15 cm)

Above:
Lion King, 2015
Ballpoint pen on paper
9 x 6 inches (23 x 15 cm)

The Chinese script, included as titles and the names of the characters in my images, are often just for a graphic appeal. They are not that important. I said what I wanted to already with the images. The Chinese writing is just worked as decoration.

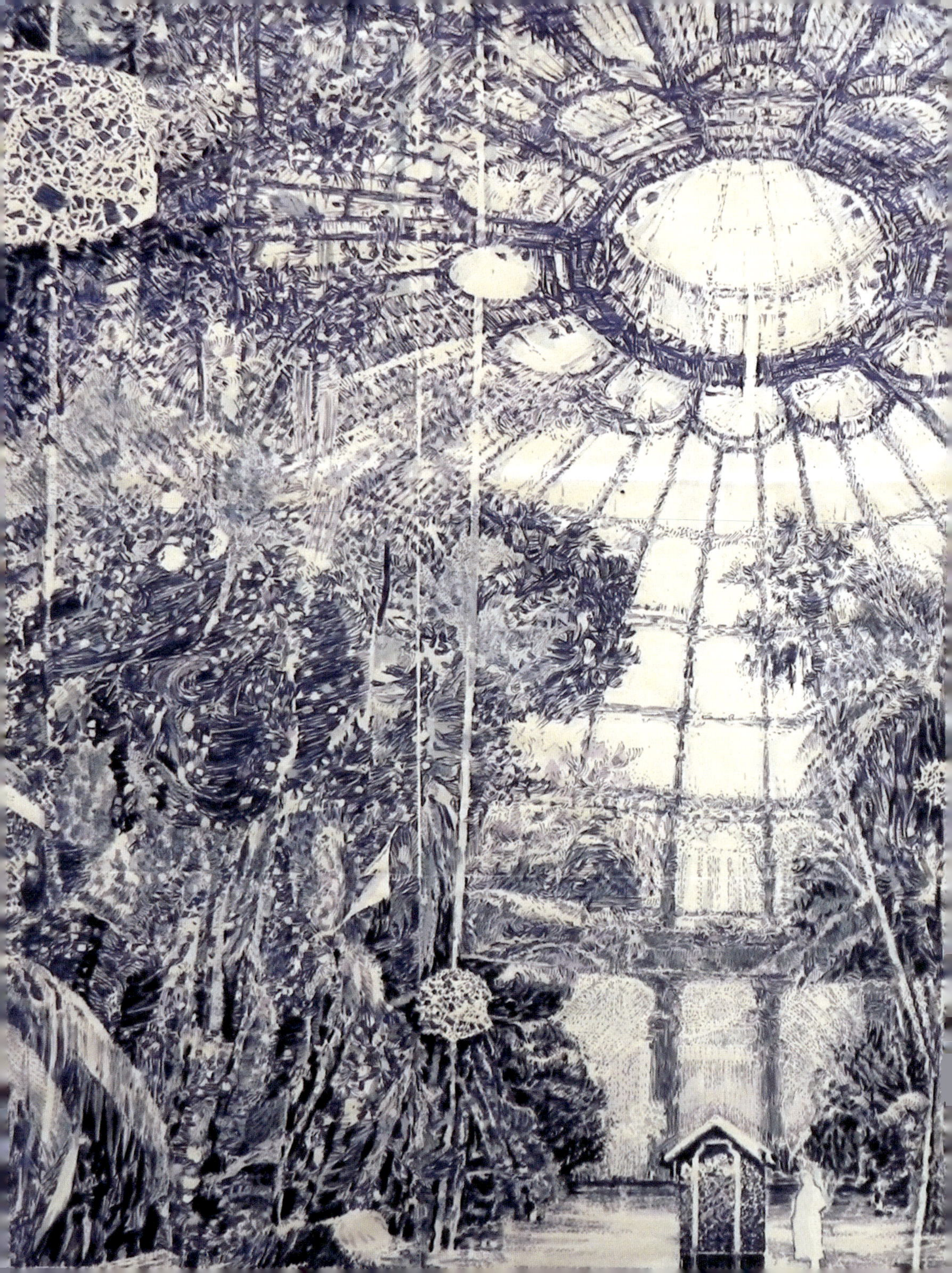

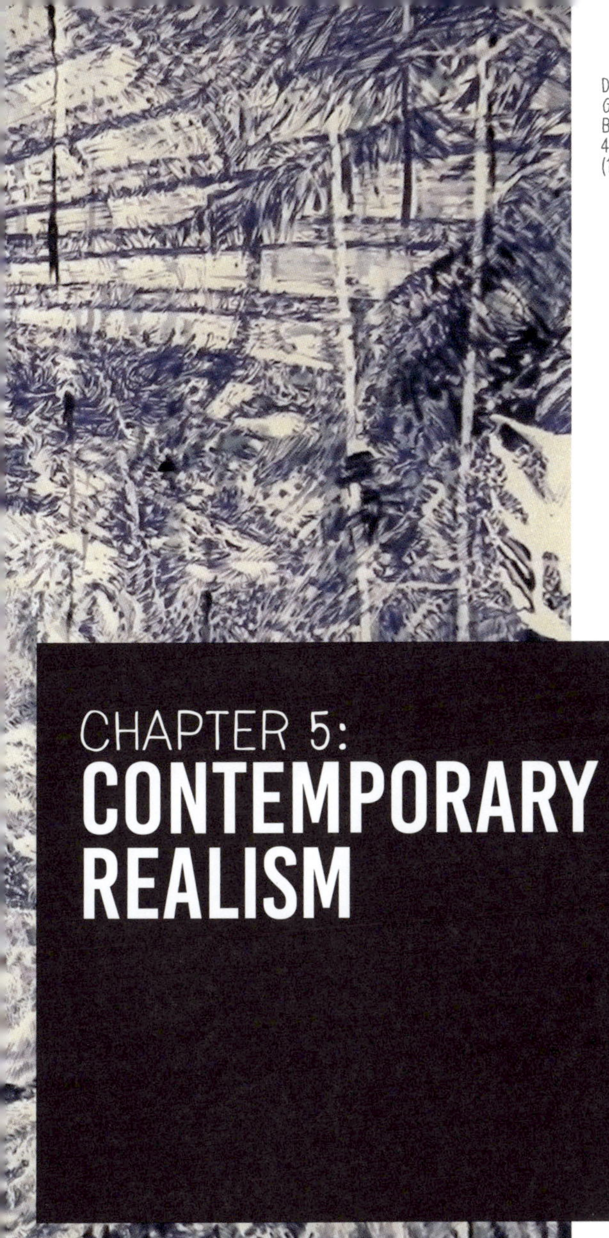

Dominique Vangilbergen
Glass House, 2011
Ballpoint pen drawing on paper
47 x 80 x 1/2 inches
(119 x 203 x 1.5 cm)

CHAPTER 5: CONTEMPORARY REALISM

Contemporary realism involves artists exploring a variety of ways of observing and representing the real world through drawing by utilizing, or even inventing new ways of, looking. Some exercises in this chapter experiment with point of view, while others focus on the act of looking closely to create an image.

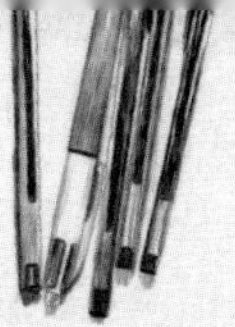

EXERCISE 17:

MULTIPLE VIEWPOINTS OF ONE OBJECT

THE PURPOSE OF THIS EXERCISE IS TO CREATE A SENSE OF TIME AND MOTION FROM A STATIONARY OBJECT.

The object itself is to remain still on a table, but you will change positions at various stages of the drawing to view the object from various angles, layering each new position on top of the next. This also will keep the drawing loose, as the drawing has to be layered. Each position cannot be overdrawn so as to leave room for the following position and subsequent layers. The drawings should overlap, but not be directly on top of each other. Every new layer will start on top of the previous and will have to deal with integrating the various positions, possibly destroying and covering up elements of the previous layer. This layering process forces you to consider the drawing, but not become attached to a single composition or pose. The process dictates the composition, so no planning can go into the composition prior to starting. In this way, you will discover an unforeseeable, unpredictable composition. This exercise separates you from any preconceived notion of a "finished" drawing or a planned composition. Rather, the composition is wholly an outcropping of, and response to, the process. The result will be a fluid and organic composition based on reacting to and building upon the previous layers.

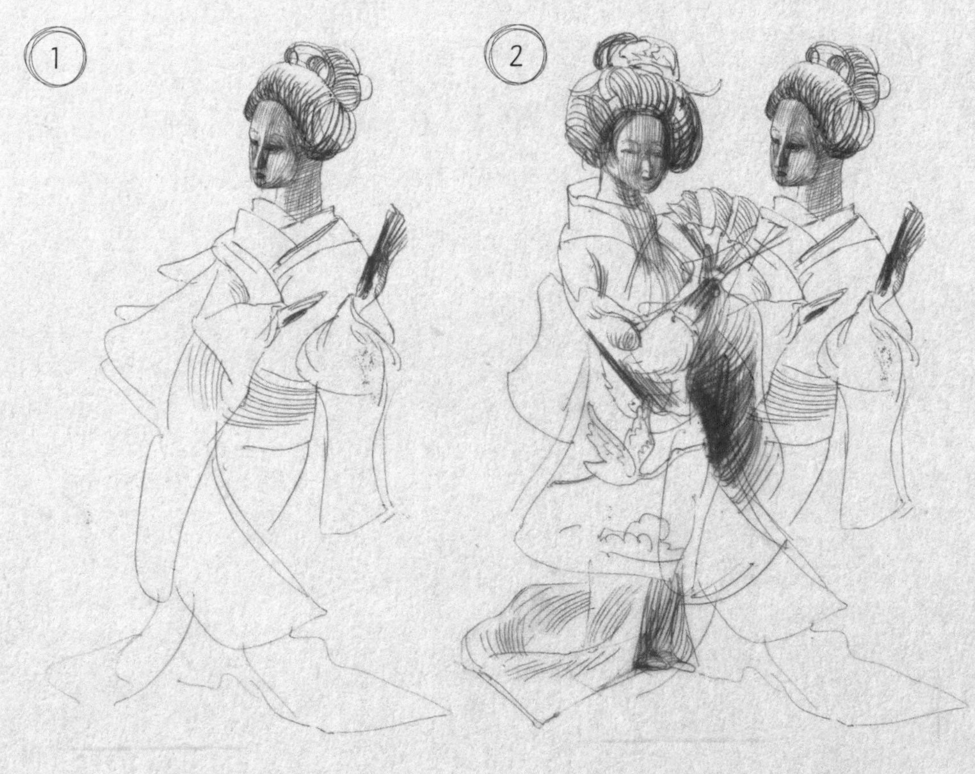
1
2

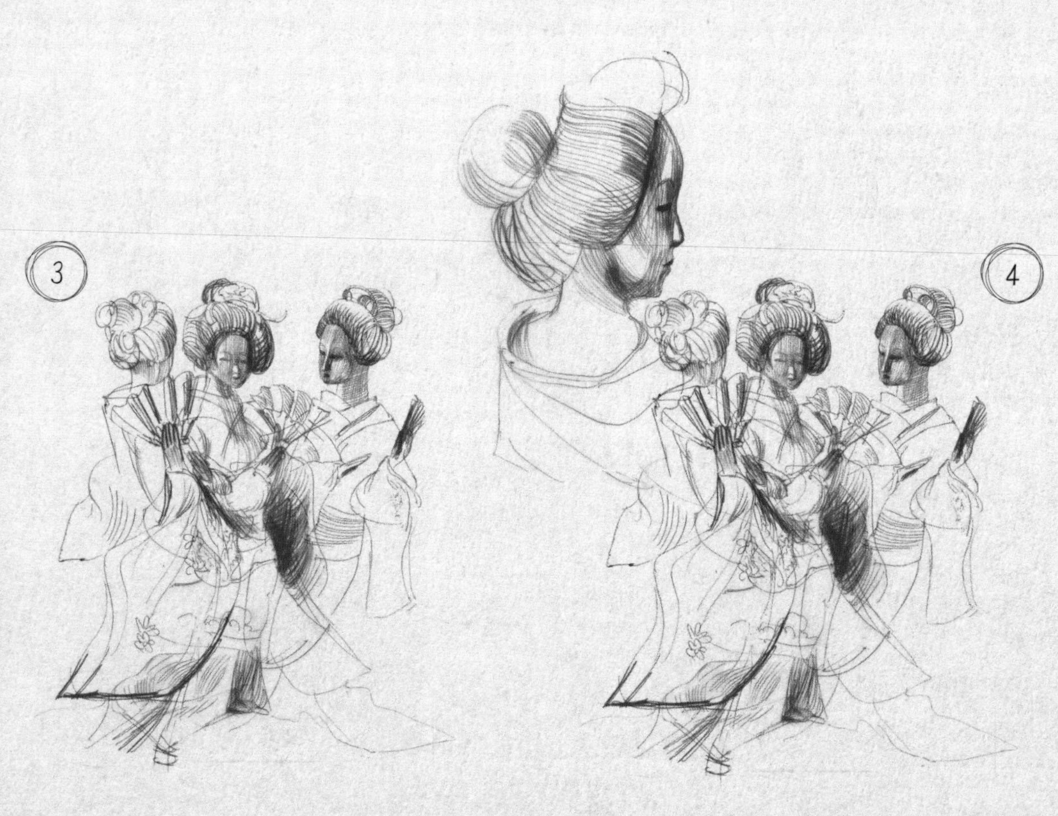
3
4

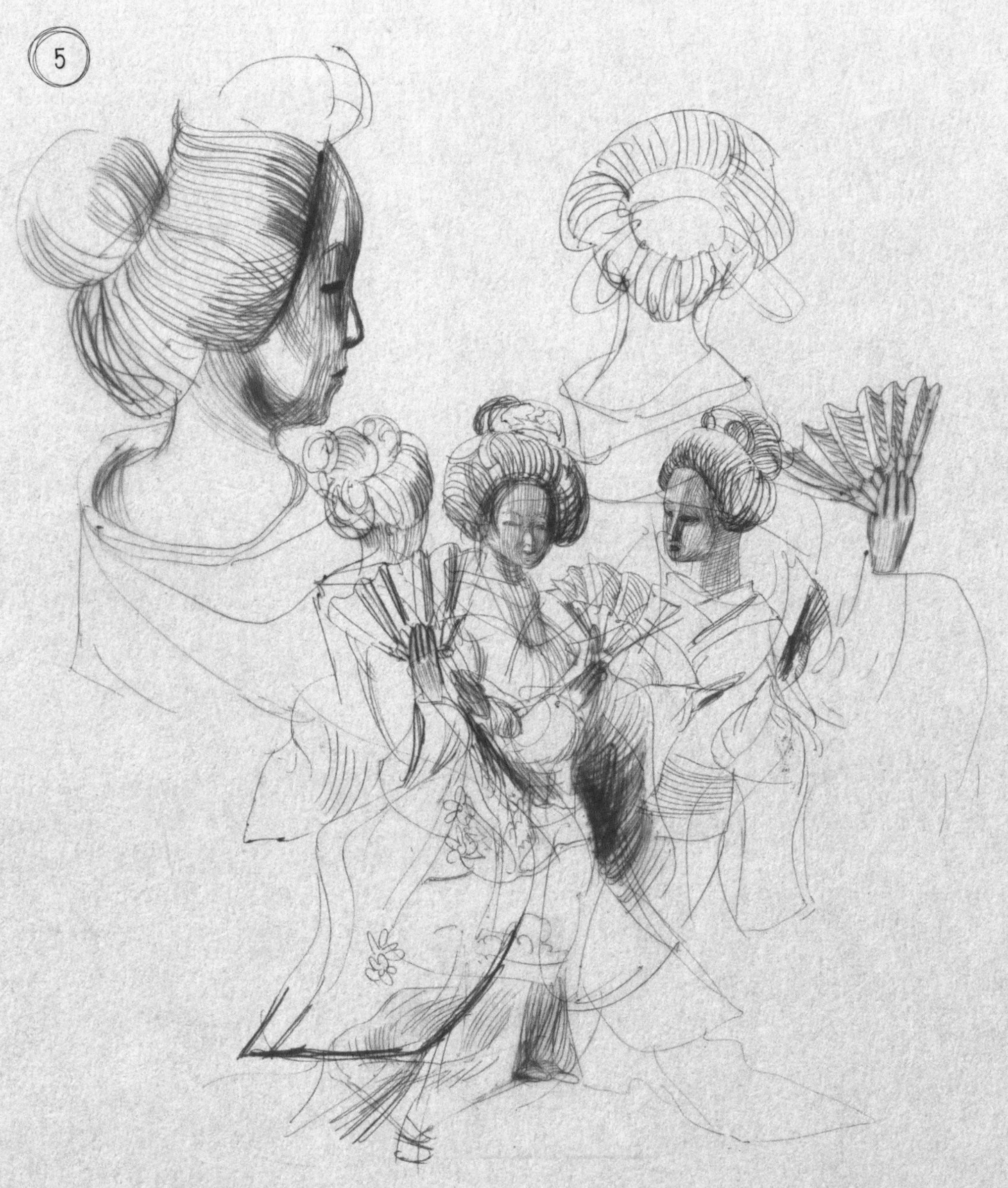
5

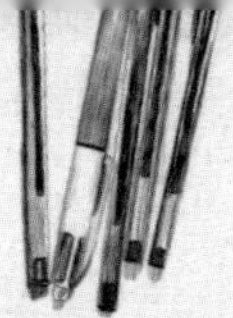

EXERCISE 18:

360-DEGREE VIEW OF A ROOM

THE OBJECT OF THIS EXERCISE IS TO CONTINUE TO ADD TO A COMPOSITION. YOU'LL START AT THE LEFT EDGE OF THE PAGE AND WORK RIGHT, CONTINUING TO ADD PAPER TO THE COMPOSITION AS THE DRAWING EXPANDS FURTHER TO THE RIGHT.

The drawing should be done in a room, and the objective is to turn in a 360-degree rotation to capture the entire space. Do not plan the drawing first and start with pen directly on the paper, without a pencil sketch.

Each page should be completed before adding on to the drawing; reworking is discouraged here. Focus only on moving across the page: think of the paper as a scroll and the drawing like writing, as if you were writing across the page and describing what you see.

The point is to not to be able to plan ahead, but to treat the drawing as a pure documentation, to draw only what is seen from that particular angle. This organic process, rather than planning, determines the composition.

Attach each page directly to the end of the last one, lined up as a continuation of the previous drawing.

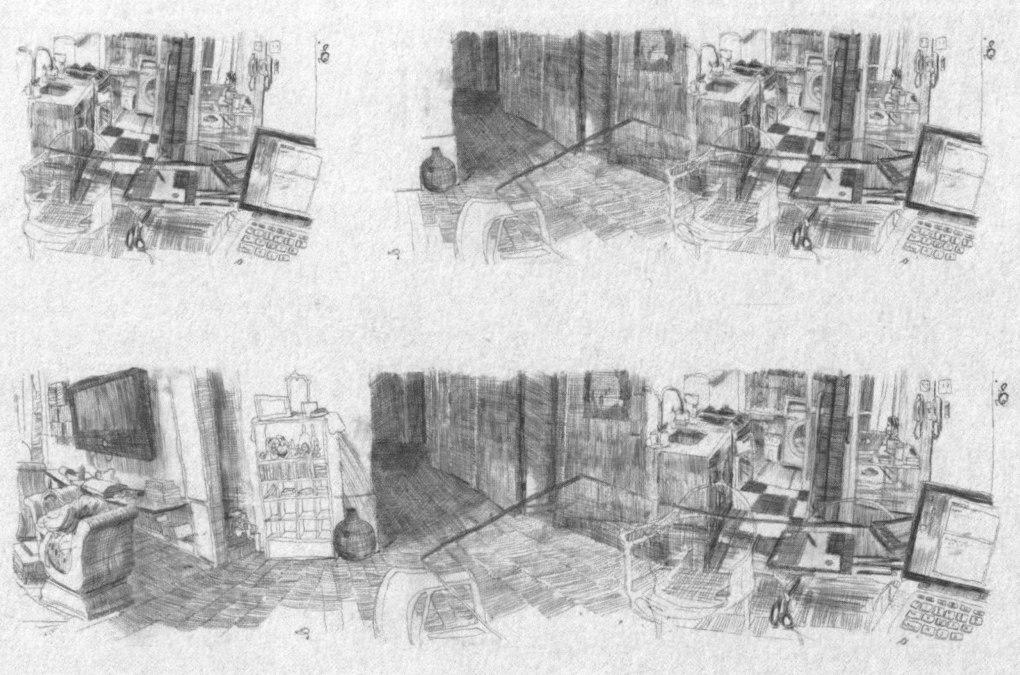

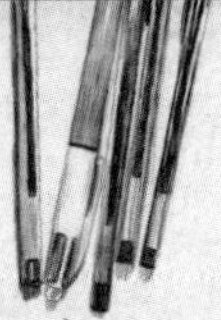

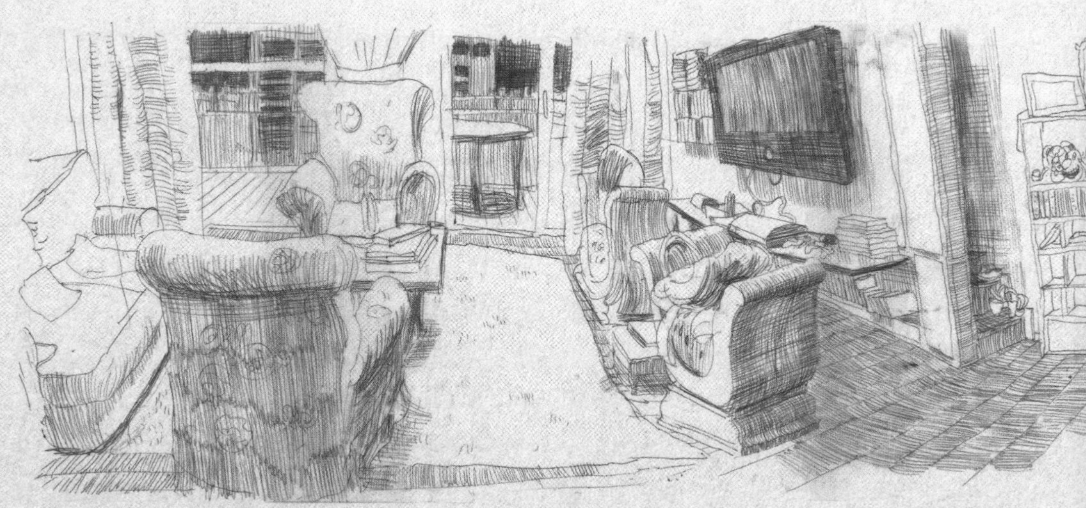

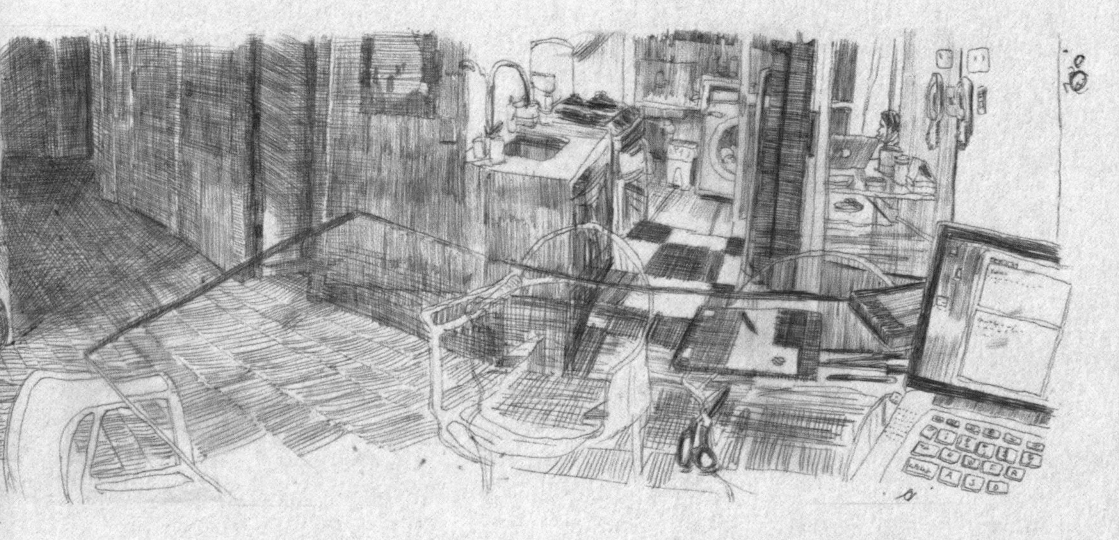

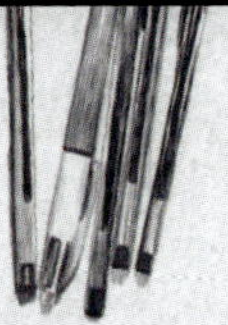

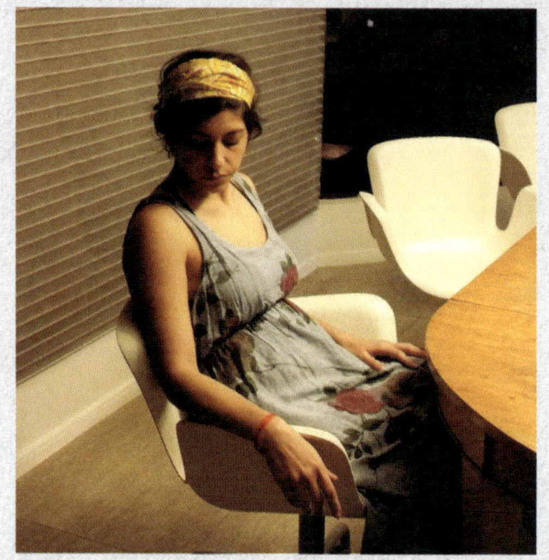

EXERCISE 19:

ONE MARK

USING ONE TYPE OF MARK FOR AN ENTIRE DRAWING FORCES THE ARTIST TO DEAL WITH LIMITATIONS. THIS ONE MARK (WHICH MOVES IN ONE DIRECTION, IN THIS CASE VERTICALLY) MUST BE USED TO DEMONSTRATE TONAL VARIATIONS AND RELATIONSHIPS BETWEEN THE COMPOSITIONAL ELEMENTS AND VARIOUS OBJECTS WITHIN THE IMAGE. IN THIS EXERCISE, THE IMAGE IS RECREATED WITH A VERTICAL DASH. THE MARK WILL STAY ROUGHLY A CONSISTENT SIZE (OTHERWISE, IT WOULD BE JUST LIKE CROSSHATCHING). WITH THIS MARK, RENDER AN ENTIRE IMAGE TONALLY.

Experiment with the mark to discover how best to create tonal variations (in this case, by clustering them tightly together for darks and using heavier marks and spacing them out for lighter tones).

It is okay to do a pencil sketch first to have an understanding of scale and proportion within the composition.

The result of this drawing will be somewhat lacking in tight detail and will be very impressionistic. There should be no outlines used with the pen (only in the preliminary pencil sketch); tonal areas intersecting will create the forms. For example, a light shape next to a dark shape will create the sense of a line. In this drawing, form is described with light and shadow, not outlines.

To understand how dark a form is, look at the space around it and determine whether the surface it is sitting on is darker or lighter than the form itself.

Start by identifying the darkest shapes and begin describing them. The shape of those forms will begin to define the negative shapes and the lighter forms.

This exercise will help create a sense of tonal relationships within a piece, as well as emphasize the "whole" image apart from its details. This process forces the artist to look and draw what is seen, rather than what is "known." A good strategy is to push the darks to be darker than they look and allow the whites to be lighter than they look.

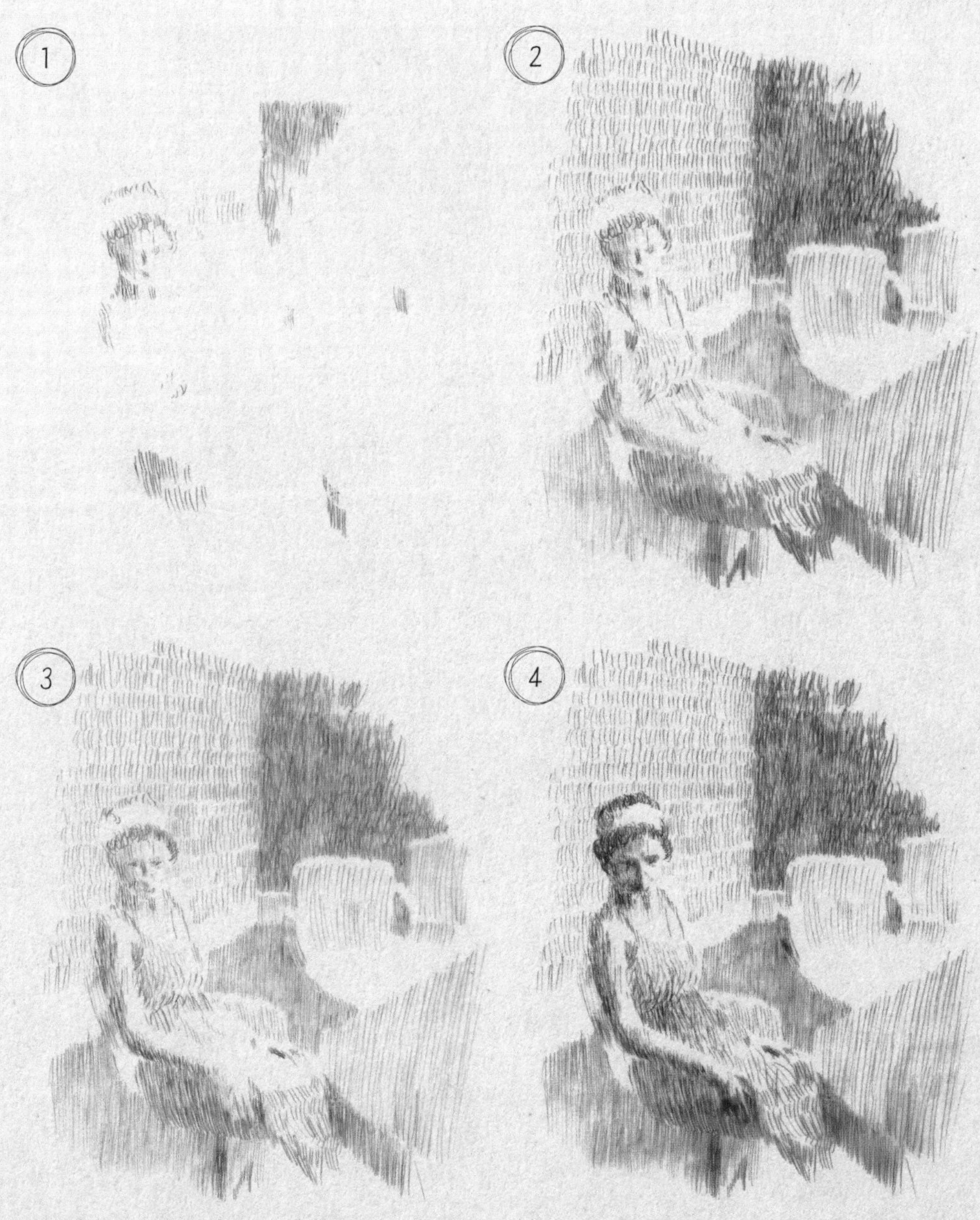
1
2
3
4

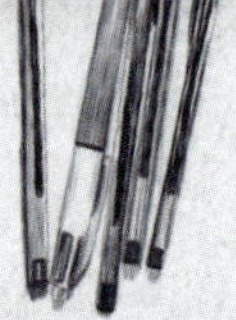

EXERCISE 20:

DRAWING TEXTURE

DRAWING TEXTURE ON AN OBJECT CAN BE INTERPRETED AS ASSIGNING A MARK THAT CAN INDICATE THE SURFACE QUALITY. THE MARK CAN BE USED TO DESCRIBE THE VOLUME AND SHAPE OF THE OBJECT. TEXTURE HELPS DIFFERENTIATE OBJECTS, SO FOR CLARITY IN A DRAWING, BEING PARTICULAR IN ASSIGNING A MARK TO DESCRIBE AN OBJECT WILL MAKE THE OBJECT FEEL UNIQUE. USING THE SAME MARK THROUGHOUT A DRAWING, OVER MANY OBJECTS, CAN GIVE THE WORK UNIFORMITY, LIKE EVERYTHING IS MADE OUT OF THE SAME MATERIAL.

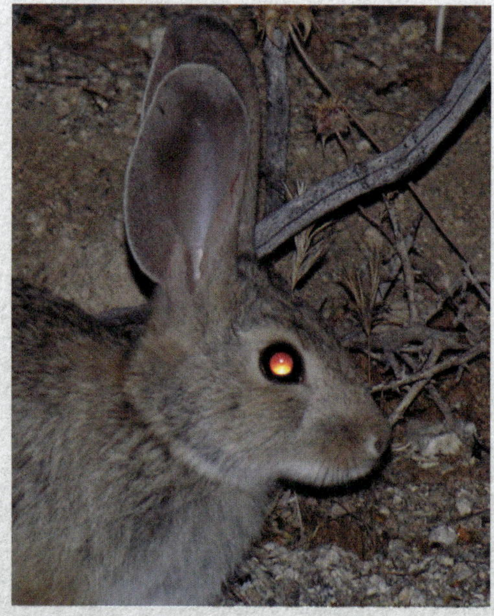

Drawing the fur of a rabbit starts off with finding the best sort of mark for the fur. Looking at the hair, a mark can be made to imitate the short curved dash. Imagine that all of the shadows on the fur are actually hundreds of little hair shadows that combine into one large shadow. When you draw the dash you are not drawing the hair so much as its shadow.

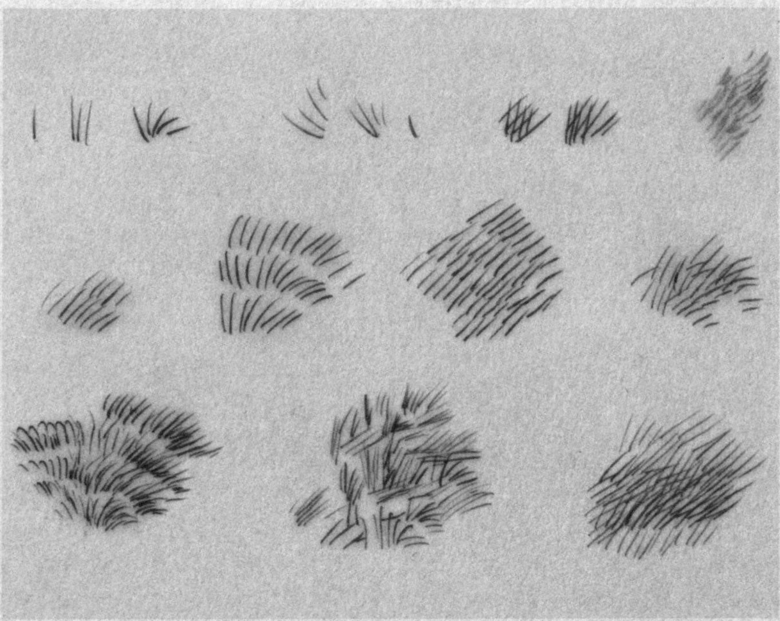

Experiment with the mark a bit before starting the drawing to find different ways of using it for shading and texture. The direction of the mark can describe how the surface curves, and layering them densely creates a darker cloud that can be used to create shadows. The evenness of the stroke describes smooth fur; drawing it in little tufts makes the hair look ruffled. These are examples of how the texture will be used to create fur for the rabbit.

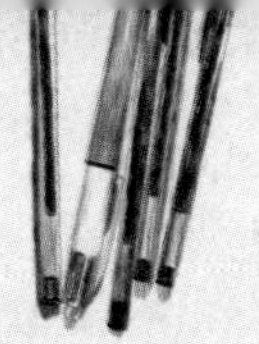

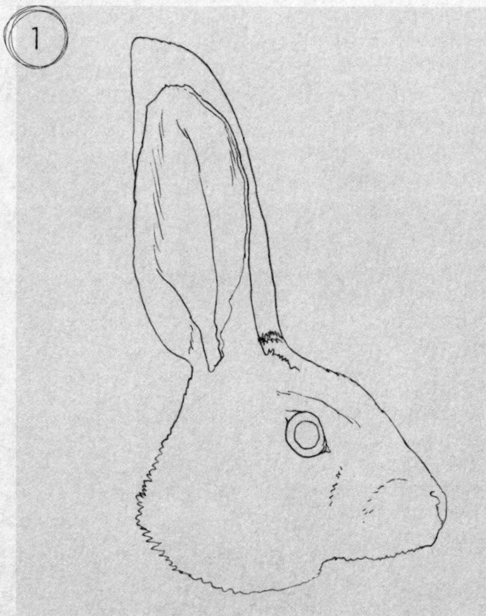

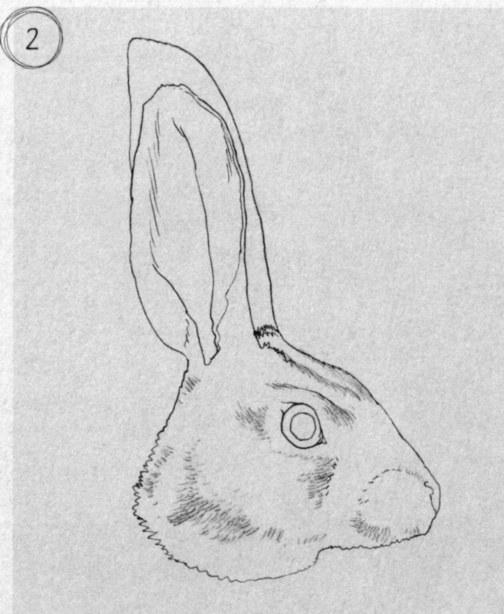

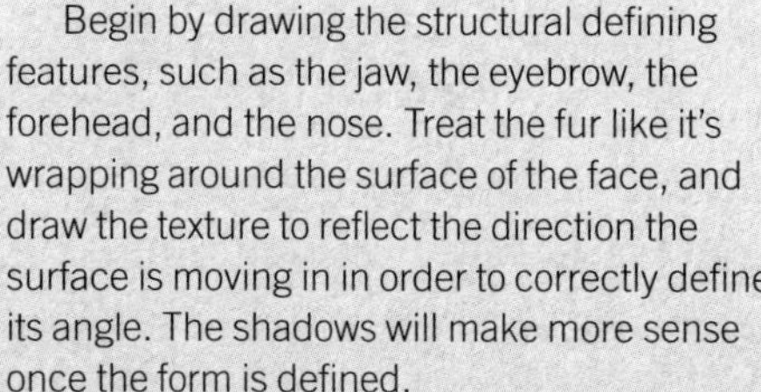

Begin by drawing the structural defining features, such as the jaw, the eyebrow, the forehead, and the nose. Treat the fur like it's wrapping around the surface of the face, and draw the texture to reflect the direction the surface is moving in in order to correctly define its angle. The shadows will make more sense once the form is defined.

Once the form is drawn, continue to spread the fur over the face, rendering the shadows. Layer the marks closer together to make the shadows darker. Avoid adding any marks for hair in the lightest area, even if you see it when examining the subject.

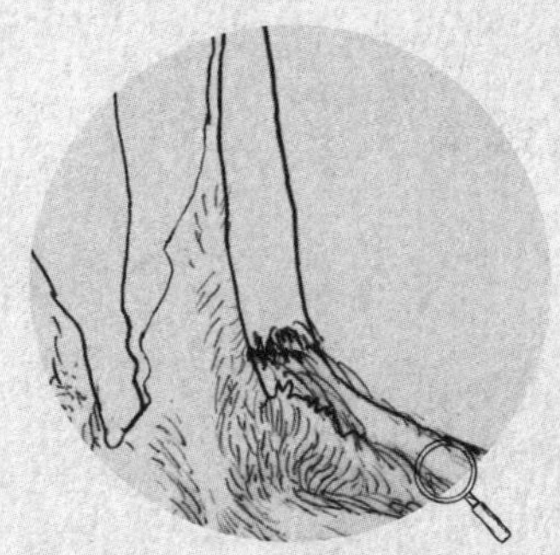

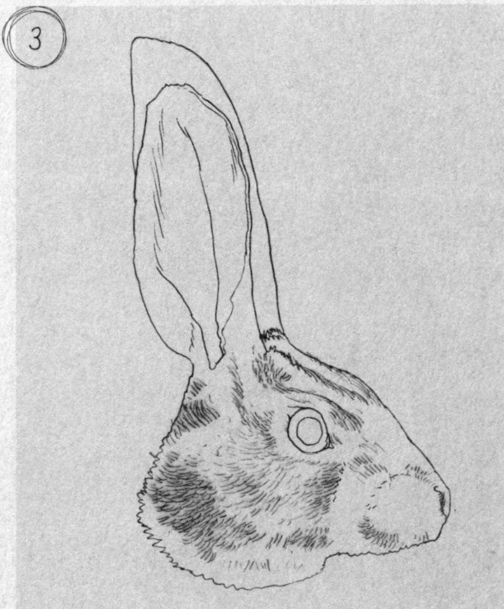

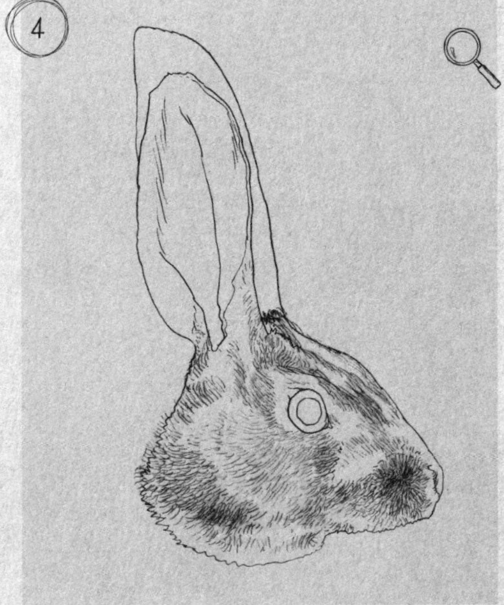

It may help to squint while looking at the rabbit so that the detail will disappear and the texture won't be visible. Look at the shapes, the dark portions that cover the surface, and describe the fur in those areas.

GALLERY: CONTEMPORARY REALISM

FEATURED ARTIST:

DOMINIQUE VANGILBERGEN

Dominique Vangilbergen views himself as a storyteller who does not tell the whole story, like an illusionist in a theater using smoke and mirrors. He chooses not to guide people through the narrative, but rather facilitates an experience that allows viewers to read into their own interpretation of the work. The objective is to suggest and evoke a mood, to stage and imply a narrative, without telling one.

Left:
Paradise Lost # 2, 2011
Ballpoint pen, charcoal, spray paint, and water color
41 x 69 x ½ inches
(104 x 175 x 1.5 cm)

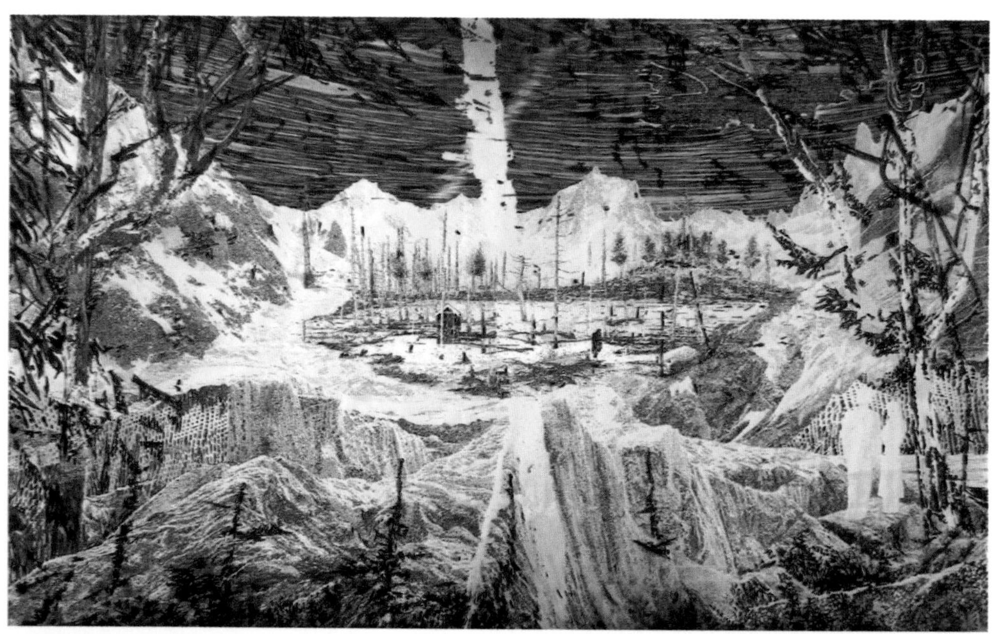

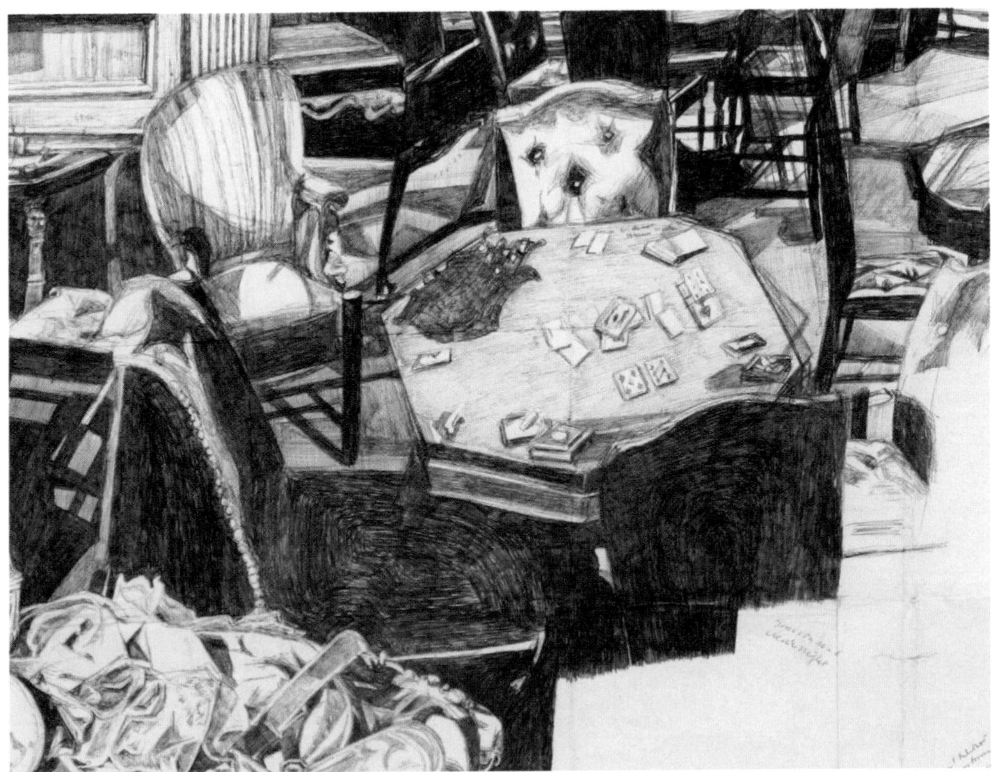

Above:
Smoking Room (Titanic, 1953), detail, 2006
Ballpoint pen on paper
42 x 78 inches
(107 x 198 cm)

FEATURED ARTIST:

DAWN CLEMENTS

Like most people, Dawn Clements uses a ballpoint pen for all kinds of writing: writing notes, making shopping lists, or doodling while on the telephone. She always has a ballpoint pen with her, which is how she started using it for her drawing. It's a natural writing, notating, and drawing tool, as well as a thinking tool. Even when there's no text in a ballpoint pen work, the very mark of ballpoint encourages "reading," not just "viewing."

FEATURED ARTIST:

JOO LEE KANG

Joo lee Kang's highly detailed renderings of mutated naturalistic subjects reference classical motifs from Victorian naturalist and decorative styles and seventeenth-century Dutch still lifes. She reinterprets the way artists have historically observed natural phenomena and plant and animal life as a form of documentation, transforming them into highly allegorical images concerned with the twenty-first century's relationship with, and manipulation of, the natural world.

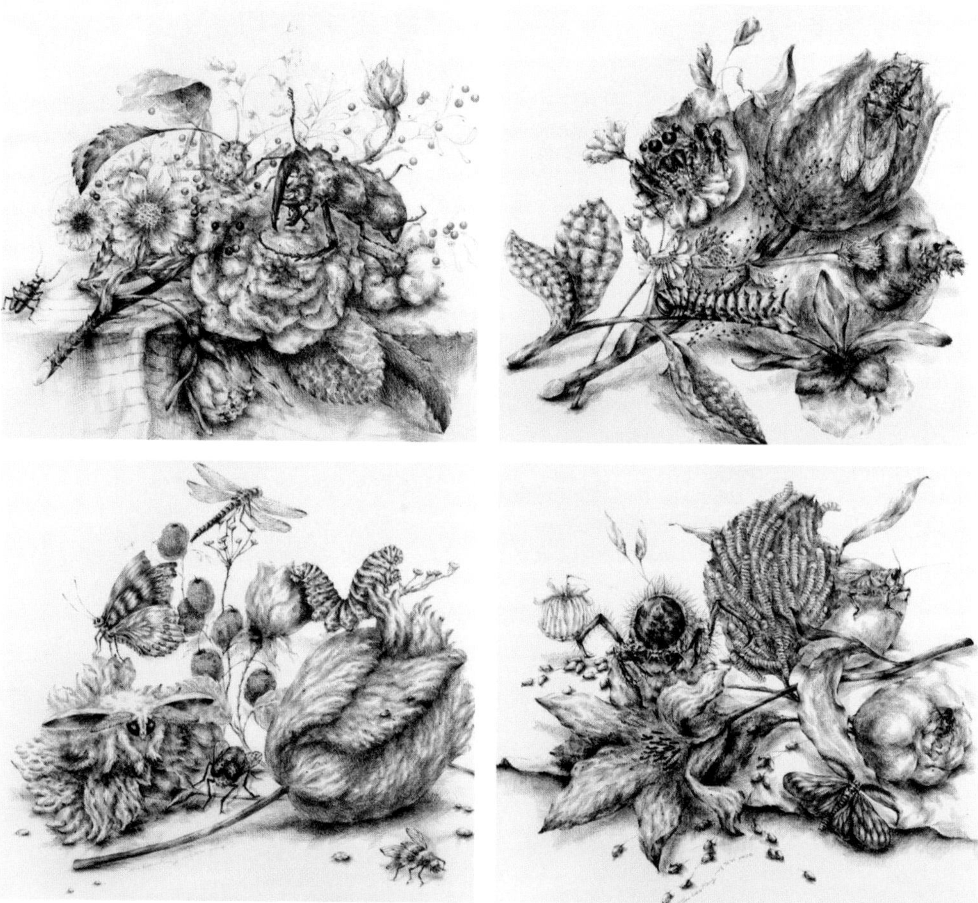

Opposite:
Still Life with Insects Series, 2014
Ballpoint pen on paper
14 x 15 inches
(35.5 x 38 cm)

Below:
Still Life with Shells #1, 2014
Ballpoint pen on paper
29½ x 40½ inches
(75 x 103 cm)

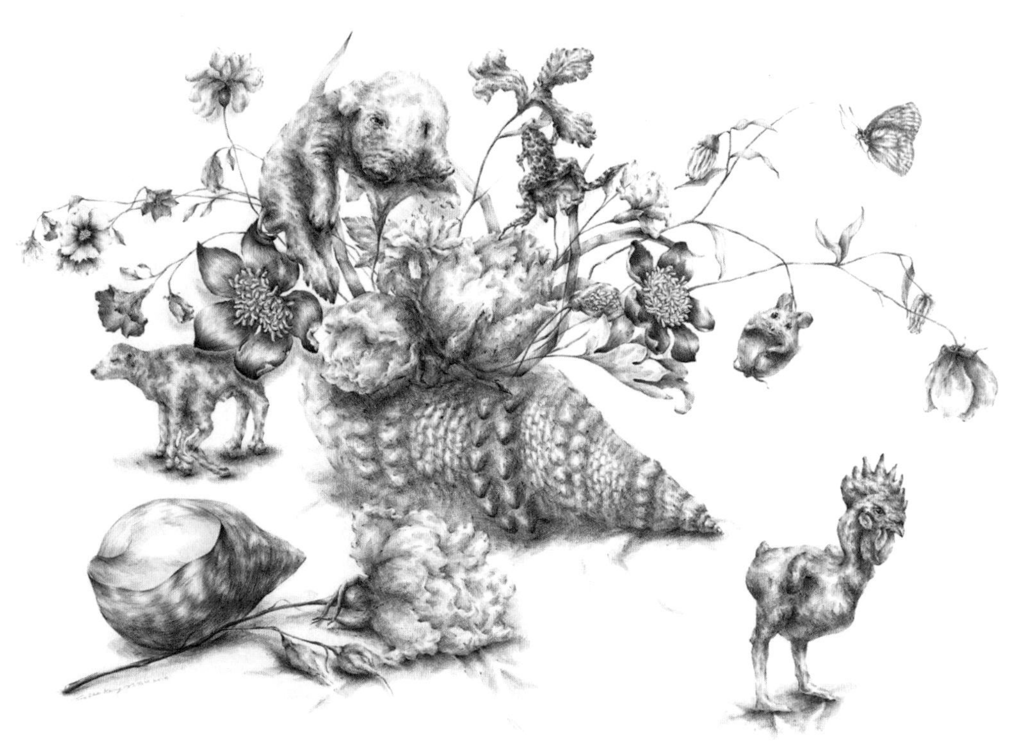

Image Highlight:

Hannah Chalew
Tree House, 2011
Pen and ink on paper
19 x 26 inches
(48.5 x 66 cm)

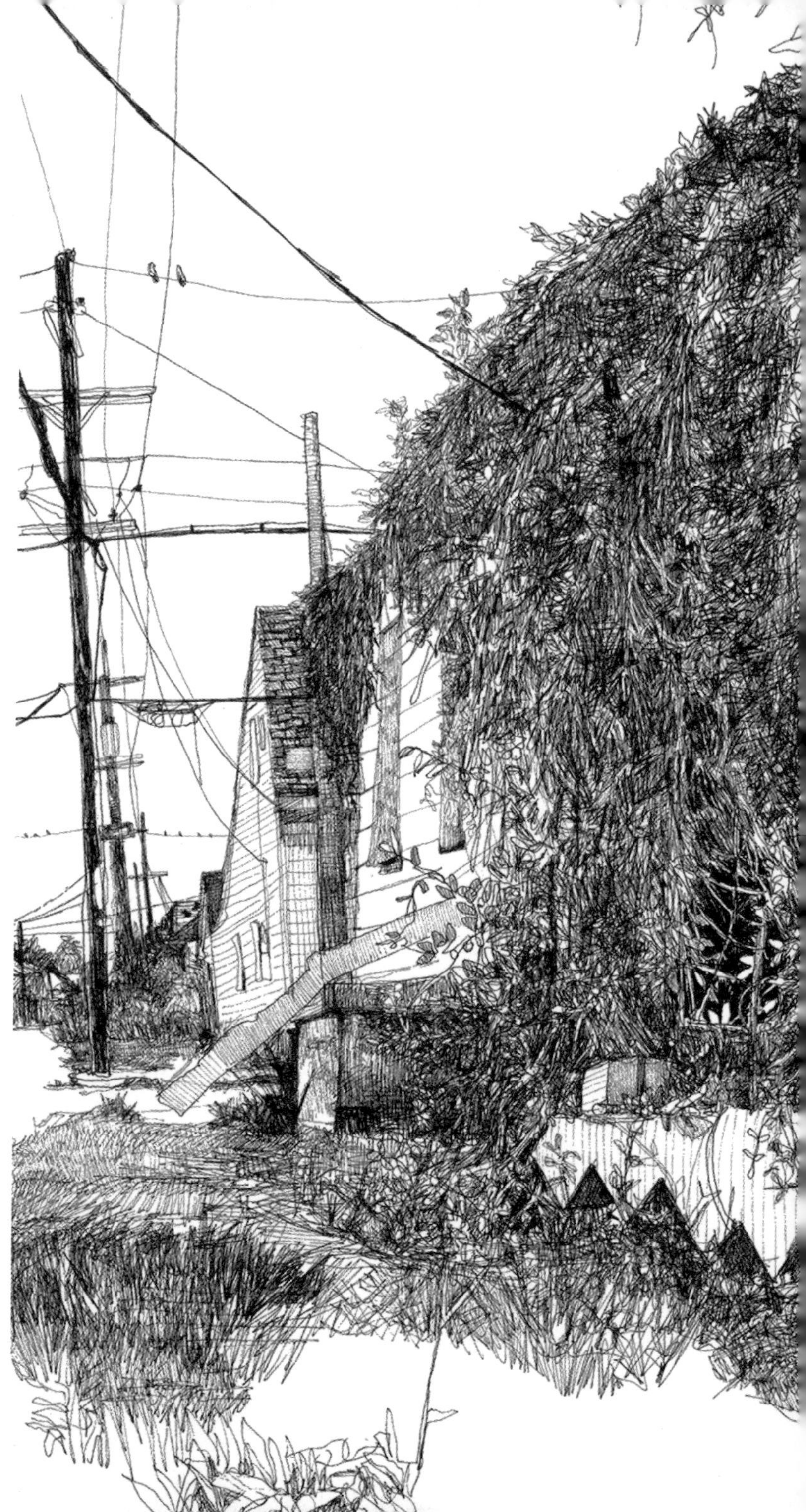

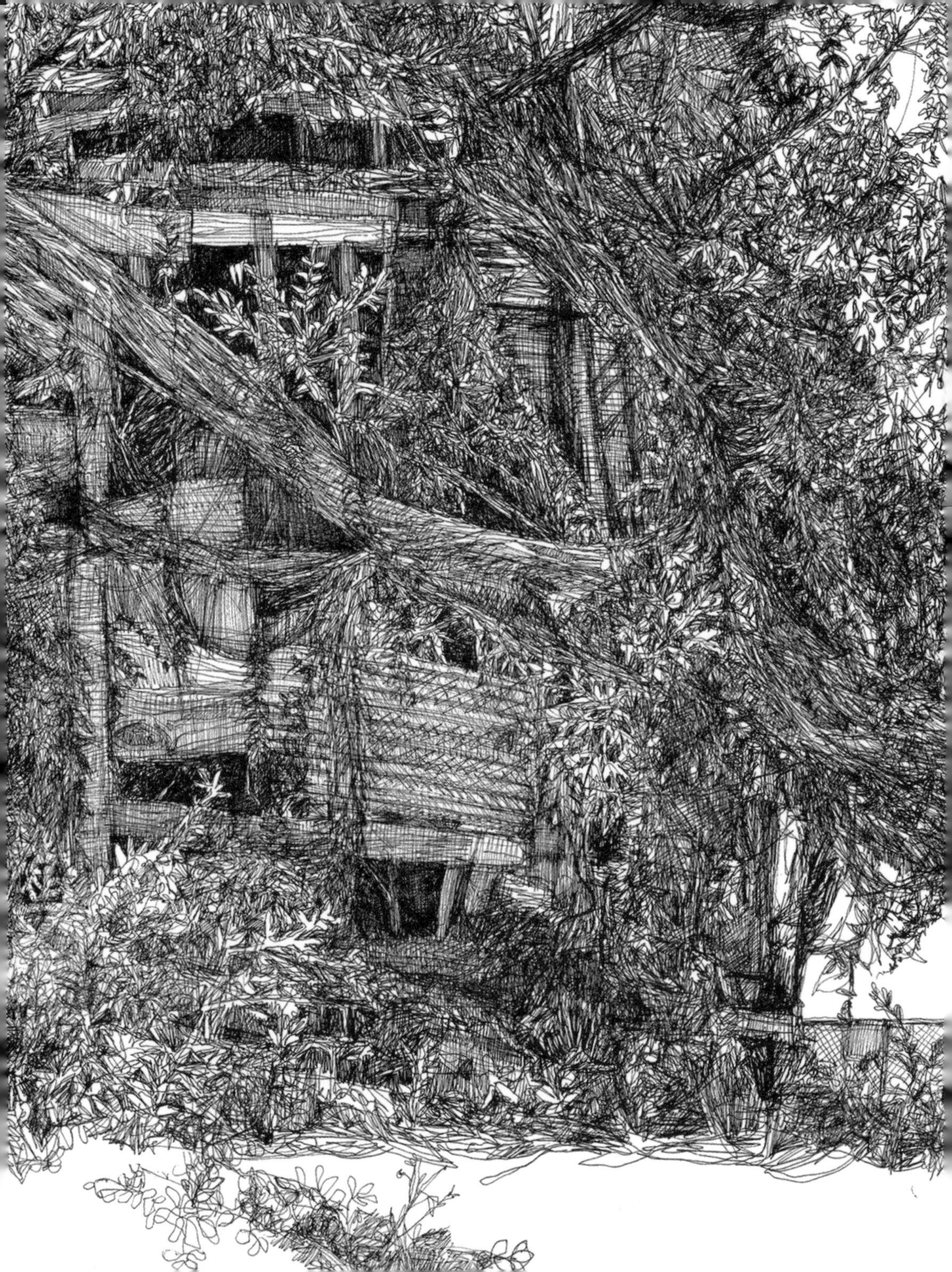

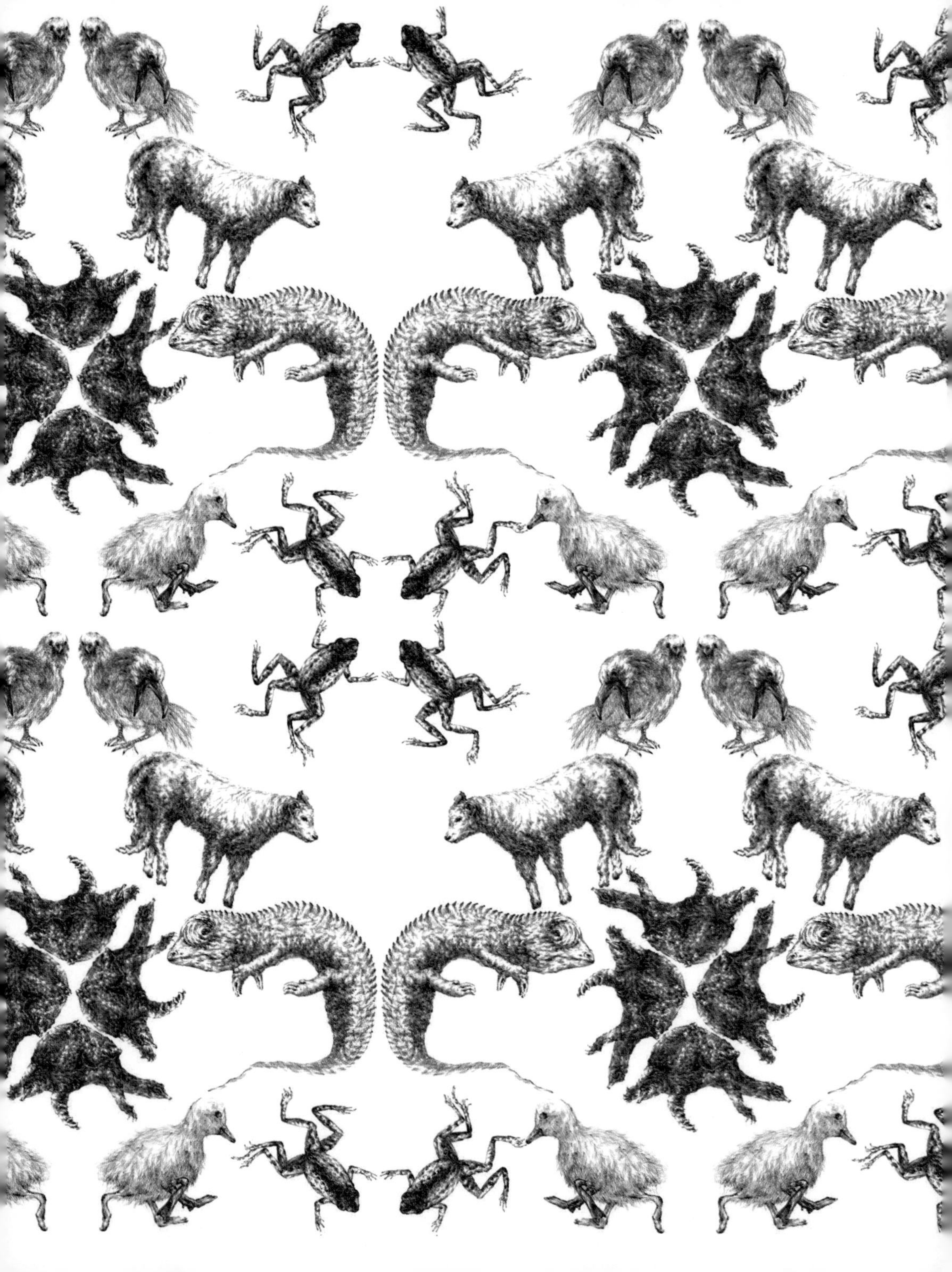

Image Highlight:
Joo Lee Kang
Pattern of Life 5, 2013
Ink-jet printed ballpoint pen-drawn wallpaper

CONTRIBUTING ARTISTS

JEAN-PIERRE ARBOLEDA
New York, USA
www.jparboleda.com

CARINE BRANCOWITZ
Paris, France
www.carinebrancowitz.com

JONATHAN BRÉCHIGNAC
Paris, France
www.joeandnathan.com

DINA BRODSKY
New York, USA
www.dinabrodsky.com

HANNAH CHALEW
New Orleans, USA
www.hannahchalew.com

JOO CHUNG
New York, USA
www.facebook.com/joo.chung.56

DAWN CLEMENTS
New York, USA
www.pierogi2000.com/artists/dawn-clements

JOANNE GREENBAUM
New York, USA
www.joannegreenbaum.com

JOO LEE KANG
Boston, USA
jooleekang.blogspot.com

MELISSA LING
New York, USA
www.melissaling.com

SHANE MCADAMS
New York, USA
www.shanemcadams.com

MU PAN
New York, USA
www.mupan.com

GUNO PARK
New York, USA
www.gunopark.com

JIM RUGG
Pittsburgh, USA
www.jimrugg.com

JOAN SALÓ
Barcelona, Spain, and Berlin, Germany
www.joansalo.net

CHAMO SAN
Barcelona, Spain
www.chamosan.com

NICOLAS V. SANCHEZ
New York, USA
www.nicolasvsanchez.com

DOMINIQUE VANGILBERGEN
Berlin, Germany
www.saatchiart.com/account/profile/291403

ACKNOWLEDGMENTS

Thank you to all of the artists that contributed; to family and friends for your help and support; and to Mary Ann and everyone at Rockport for your help, and for making this book such a fun process.

ABOUT THE AUTHOR

Matt Rota is a New York artist specializing in narrative technique with watercolor, ink, and digital media. He currently teaches at the School of Visual Arts' graduate Visual Narrative program in New York City and has taught in the illustration department at the Maryland Institute College of Art in Baltimore. His clients include *The New York Times, McSweeney's,* the *Washington Post, Foreign Policy* magazine, *Smithsonian* magazine, Chronicle Books, *Vice, ProPublica, Matter,* the *Boston Globe, GQ Italy*, and other publications. He has worked on the films *Resurrect Dead* and *A Late Quartet*. His drawings and prints have been exhibited at the National Arts Club, the Society of Illustrators, and Last Rites Gallery in New York; the Copro Gallery in Los Angeles; Galerie L'Oeil du Prince in Paris; and several other international locations. His comics have been anthologized in print and online in *Rabid Rabbit, Amazing Forest, Top Shelf 2.0,* and *Study Group*. He has received recognition and awards from *American Illustration, Communication Arts, 3x3* magazine, *Creative Quarterly, Spectrum*, and Lürzer's Int'l Archive, where he was listed as one of the top 200 illustrators worldwide. Matt was awarded a silver medal by the Society of illustrators.